INSIDE TIMMY'S MIND

ENTER AT YOUR OWN RISK

TIMMY BOYLE

To:
MARCIE &
RANDI
KEEP ON
LAUGHIN'!
T

BREATH OF FRESH AIR PRESS

Inside Timmy's Mind
Published by Breath of Fresh Air Press
PO Box 12, St Clair NSW 2759
Australia
www.breathoffreshairpress.com.au

Cover Design by Steve Ariss
www.arissberg.com

Illustrations by Dave Coleman
www.theagsc.com

Layout by Breath of Fresh Air Press

ISBN: 978-1-922135-02-5 (paperback)

National Library of Australia Cataloguing-in-Publication entry

Author:	Boyle, Timmy, author.
Title:	Inside Timmy's Mind / by Timmy Boyle; Illustrations byDave Coleman
ISBN:	9781922135025 (paperback)
Dewey Number:	808.879811

Acknowledgements

To Heidi, my wife and princess, for always believing in my writings and for simply allowing me to be me.

To my awesome children — Jade, Aliyah and Connor —for providing an opportunity to pass on my wisdom to future generations . . . without having to write it down.

To Jeanine, my mom and biggest fan, who will brag about me whether I'm writing a book or eating a ham sandwich.

To my father and greatest role model, John, for genetically imparting the sarcastic wit of the Irish deep within me . . . now flowing out through these pages.

To Wil, a friend and fellow comedian, for introducing me to FaithWriters . . . which ultimately led to the publishing of my mind.

To the second half of my mind, Steve, for letting me tap into his creative genius (over and over) . . . and for capturing the pure essence of "Timmy" in the cover photo.

To Dave, the artist behind the brilliant sketches, who successfully transported me into the cartoon world . . . from which many people believe I came in the first place.

To my amazing publisher and editor, Deb, who saw something special enough in me and my writings to take a risk . . . which I hope proves to have been no risk at all.

And finally, to Ben Stiller and Alyssa Milano . . . for just being them.

What's Inside . . .

Timmy's Mind

INTRODUCTION

"If you don't have anything good to say . . .
don't let people know you said it."
~ ANONYMOUS ~

Do the following questions ever pop up in your mind?

* Did people really land on the moon?
* Is there a God?
* How have The Rolling Stones lived so long?

Well, this book answers none of them. However, if you've ever wondered . . .

* is the grass really greener on Mercury?
* aren't all the gifts of the *Twelve Days of Christmas* just a little too much?
* how can getting "just desserts" be a bad thing?

. . . then you must buy this book right now!

And if you have ever . . .

* cursed technology, snickered at psychics, or cringed at the sight of Speedos®;
* been sick, gone on vacation, or made a mistake; or
* wondered why phonics only seems to apply to half the English language . . .

. . . then this book just has to be in your bathroom reading basket today!

If you've never read . . .

* heated dialogue between a person and a colour;
* inspired poetry about Big Bird or Hulk Hogan;
* about a day in the life of a hall monitor . . .

. . . then this book absolutely must be the centerpiece on your coffee table.

From colourful conversations to hilarious timelines and absurd scenarios, *Inside Timmy's Mind* is a journey through the ordinary with an extraordinary perspective, bringing laughter every step of the way.

You will discover intriguing stories:

"It seemed to revolve around free-range chickens, Abe Lincoln, and a road trip to Kamloops, BC."

*

"It's been exactly ten years since my family and I first settled into our remote, northern Manitoba bunker. I bet Mr. Y2K-is-a-bunch-of-malarkey wishes he'd listened to me now."

*

"We arrive home only to find our house burnt to the ground by those pesky Vikings. Luckily, my wife was safe, as she had been hiding under the haystack where we kept the key to our barn."

You will ponder curious statements:

* "Sure, you can bring your unicorn over."
* "Hey, kid! Get Daddy another bon-bon."

* "More relational accidents happen in the washroom than any other room in the house."

You will delve into deep concepts:

"After an intense search, Brain was discovered, curled up in fetal position, fast asleep. Brain's waves were as flat as the voice of an eliminated *American Idol* contestant."

*

"I haven't slept in three weeks, my arms and shoulders are numb, and I've got poop under my fingernails, but I know what my baby is saying. It's heaven."

*

"Tuesday is a day of frenetic activity, with two days' work needing to be done in one, mainly because most people spent Monday moping, dragging their feet, and cursing the day's very existence."

Inside Timmy's Mind is insightful, inspirational, and downright hilarious! It is, by far, one of the most dynamic books of the 21st Century. A must read for every literate person.

From the Author . . .

I really hope you buy this book . . . because my children need to eat.

Actually, if you've read this far—and haven't yet arranged a book burning ceremony—it probably means you'll thoroughly enjoy what's on the following pages.

According to the experts, a book introduction should ultimately answer the question, "Why should I buy this?" I will admit to giving consideration to offering you empty, yet intriguing, promises like . . .

* 100 secrets to great wealth by doing nothing!
* 76 tips for a happy marriage . . . while staying selfish.
* 4 steps to lose 100 pounds on a chocolate only diet.

However, I decided to answer the question by being real. Despite how hungry my children may be, I have no desire to get you to spend your hard-earned money on false pretenses.

If the introduction made you laugh out loud, chuckle mildly, smile, or at the very least grin, then take this book home right now. If you have enjoyed the snapshots, you'll enjoy the journey even more.

If the introduction has made you uncomfortable, slightly confounded, or a little queasy, then buy this book for a friend who has a sense of humour — if for no other reason than you don't want my kids to starve.

Simply put, I'm a fairly normal guy who just happens to see life through fairly odd lenses.

Inside Timmy's Mind is a collection of my favorite short essays, written with the sole purpose of making people laugh. I hope you'll enjoy reading my unique perspectives and absurd ideas as much as I enjoyed writing them.

TIMMY BOYLE
November, 2013

(P.S. I wrote the quote at the beginning of this introduction.)

WARNING

ALTHOUGH YOU CAN'T CATCH INSANITY, POSSIBLE SIDE EFFECTS INCLUDE:

* MILK SPOUTING FROM YOUR NOSE;
* LOSS OF BLADDER CONTROL; AND
* A TEMPORARY ENJOYMENT OF LIFE

ENTER AT OWN RISK

A Shift in the Life of a Hall Monitor

Recently, our church instituted a plan to create a safer environment for the children who attend our Sunday morning program. As a result, many new roles have been created.

I am now Hall Monitor Timmy, but you can call me Sir.

I take my job *very* seriously. The safety of our children is at stake.

With the eyes of a hawk and the reflexes of a cat, I monitor a hall like no other. I give you fair warning. Do not cross the man in orange!

10:10 a.m. Starting my warm-up. A few stretches and one lap of the hall. People are watching and they look impressed. I'm not sure if it's because of my level of commitment or my pink leg warmers.

10:15 a.m. Heading to gymnasium to sign in. Will practice my "tough guy" walk on the way.

10:17 a.m. Was "bumped" three times in the hall. Thank goodness for self-control.

10:19 a.m. Just picked up my shirt and name tag. The name tag is fine, but the shirt is orange. That would not have been my number one choice. When I mentioned this to the woman behind the table she called me a diva, tossed me the shirt (with some oomph), and told me to get to work. Thanks, Mom.

10:22 a.m. Setting up my Control Centre.

10:24 a.m. Just had four people tell me that calling a chair a "Control Centre" is a little over the top.
Hey, Pastor, thanks so much for that sermon last week on speaking truth.

10:29 a.m. One minute 'til lockdown. Washrooms? Clear! Classrooms? Clear! Air Ducts? Clear!

10:30 a.m. This hallway is now the safest place in the world. The President of the United States could wander freely . . . if he had three pieces of ID.

10:35 a.m. I have to go to the bathroom, but no worries. Depends®.

10:44 a.m. Just had my first situation. The person entered my hallway and proceeded to reach into their pocket. In that type of situation, it's kill or be killed. I had no choice but to respond with a quick arm-bar takedown.

10:45 a.m. False alarm.
Turns out she was getting a mint.
I helped her up, told her to keep both hands visible next time, and returned her cane.

10:51 a.m. Some guy keeps knocking at the door, and it's getting *very* annoying.

10:58 a.m. He's gone . . . finally! The man was persistent, but I just stared ahead and pretended I couldn't hear him. Next week he'll come on time.

11:00 a.m. It's almost time for the sermon, and a deacon just asked if I'd seen the pastor. Apparently he stepped out for a second . . . some time ago. Maybe he's counselling the latecomer.

11:05 a.m. Children's program is about to split-up into their separate class rooms. Have to go monitor the changeover.

11:10 a.m. Didn't like the way one of the kids looked at me. I've removed him from the group until I can cross-reference his name tag with the attendance list.

11:12 a.m. All clear, but I will certainly be addressing that disrespectful look . . . once we get home.

11:15 a.m. Have to go to the bathroom. No worries.

11:18 a.m. Ushers are coming through with the offering plates. My adrenaline is pumping faster than Santa's sleigh on Christmas Eve.

11:22 a.m. I kept them safe. No tip.

11:25 a.m. Little girl pinched her finger in a chair. Looks pretty bad. I have to get ice.

11:32 a.m. Stop crying already! I'll get ice once I've finished double-checking all the doors and blind spots.

11:35 a.m. When I gave her the ice the little girl started laughing. I thought it was because her finger was feeling better, but it was actually because she thought my outfit was funny looking. Apparently, my orange shirt doesn't go very well with the pink leg warmers.
No kidding, Sherlock! Orange wasn't my first pick, either.

12:00 p.m. Service is running late, but I will not abandon my post.

12:10 p.m. C'mon! *Seriously.*

12:14 p.m. That fifteenth repeat of the chorus has just cost you overtime pay.

12:17 p.m. *Finally!* I was getting nervous. My Depends® are not holding up well.

12:25 p.m. Returned my name tag and shirt. I gently placed the tag on the table and tossed the shirt back to Mom . . . with some oomph.
Not a good plan.

12:29 p.m. Have to pack up my Control Centre and then head off to a meeting. I'm told the pastor wants to see me. Probably wants to extend his personal congratulations.
Just doing my job, Pastor. Just doing my job.

Halloween Cheer; Christmas Fear

Earlier this week I was out shopping . . . well, "shopping" may be a bad choice of words because I wasn't planning to purchase anything.

So, earlier this week I was out looking in stores.

No . . . I don't think "looking" is right, either because there wasn't anything that I was seeking out in particular.

Earlier this week I was blindly following my wife through a variety of stores.

Yeah. That's better.

Anyways, while on the journey, I had to navigate through aisle after aisle after aisle of Halloween merchandise. Not surprising, of course. Being October and all, 'tis the season.

Admittedly, I am not a big fan of this particular holiday. I wouldn't describe myself as a Halloween Scrooge or anything; I just don't go out of my way to acknowledge its existence. For me, death, blood, and gore have never been overly appealing.

Now, I know it's not all dark, for there will be many bunnies, Transformers, and lil' Taylor Swifts walking the streets. However, the cute will still be severely outnumbered by the demons, zombies, and lil' Robert Pattinsons.

Creepy!

Also, it's not like Halloween has a whole lot to offer me. I mean, I can get my hands on candy whenever I please, and

I play "dress-up" more than enough over a calendar year to get my fill.

So, as I weaved through the crowd, trying to keep up with my wife, it should really be no surprise that I wasn't paying attention to the ghoulish masks, pumpkin lanterns, and tomb stones with witty sayings like . . . "R.I.P." (not that witty).

But at one point I stopped dead in my tracks, which is a very appropriate phrase, given the season and all that.

My jaw dropped. A cloud of dread and fear came over me.

I was paralyzed.

I even tried calling out to Heidi, who had continued on without me, but I couldn't utter a sound.

I had never felt so . . . trapped.

It was the most horrifying sight—and I'm not talking about the XXXL French Maid costume, which was certainly very disturbing, as well.

No.

Down the next aisle was . . .

was . . .

was . . .

CHRISTMAS DECORATIONS.

Noooooooooooooooooooooooooooooooo!

Jeepers creepers. Can't we at least get through one holiday before moving on to the next? I mean, do we really need two full months to prepare for Christmas . . . or any holiday for that matter?

It was bad enough when garland and fruit cake started to surface on November 1, but now stores are selling fake snow almost a week before Halloween.

On the sixty-first day of Christmas,
my true love gave to me . . .
sixty-one skeletons a dancin'

The end is near, folks. Take that big rubber knife (from aisle four) and drive it deep into my fake heart (from aisle three).

For the next few minutes, I stumbled around like a zombie, in complete disbelief. As much as I like Santa, and all, I cringed more at the sight of that jolly ol' elf than I did at the creepy man with the loose eyeball.

Now I fear the very thought of entering the mall on December 14 and having to navigate aisles brimming with gifts for Valentine's Day! If that happens, be assured there will be no love flowing from me. Christmas cheer . . . yes. Love . . . no.

Maybe the stores should just stock their shelves for every holiday, twelve months a year. Ghosts, reindeer, Cupid . . . oh my!

Or maybe they should merge them into one big holiday. All day, every day: "Happy Consumerism."

Someone, please stop this holiday madness. It's making me so sick I just dropped a rubber puddle of vomit on the floor.

The People on Mercury Have it so Good

I really wish I had more time in a day. But then, who doesn't? *The Mercurians!* That's who.

Already blessed with the best tropical climate this side of the sun, the inhabitants of Mercury get 4,224 hours every day to live life to the fullest.

Over 4,000 hours . . .

. . . *a day!*

I'm so ridiculously jealous.

Can you imagine having that much time to accomplish your daily routines? Here's what I'd do:

1. Sleep

   I will acknowledge the obvious temptation to pull an all-nighter, but that would be foolish. By the 3,500-hour mark I'd start to lose focus and my production level would drop-off significantly.

   You see, certain universal laws apply, regardless of which planet you inhabit. On Mercury, as on Earth, the key to achieving peak daily effectiveness is getting the proper rest.

   Earth doctors recommend seven to nine hours a day. So, if my math is right, Mercurians are probably looking to get double that, at least. Taking into account my penchant for sleeping in, that would allow:

Time for Sleep	20.0 hours
Time Remaining	4,204.0 hours

2. EXERCISE

No more excuses. Exercise would finally become the priority I've always intended it to be.

At present, I set aside thirty to sixty minutes a day to maintain my fitness level. But as I'm getting older, I'm recognizing the need to increase my dedication level if I want to actually combat the aging process.

Jack LaLanne would have *loved* Mercury.

However, I am not about to foolishly strive for something unrealistic. Sure, it's intriguing to think how ripped my abs would be if I set aside 1,000 hours a day to Wii Fit™, but who needs to be that big . . . or spend that much on batteries? I'm more than happy just being healthy and toned.

So, factoring in time to turn on the Wii™, change batteries, and shower, that would give me:

Time for Exercise	528.0 hours
Time Remaining	3,676.0 hours

3. EAT

Initially, I had thought about abandoning all time-saving meals, like Kraft Dinner® and Minute® Rice, but unless the Mercury currency exchange rate is a 1,700 percent increase on my dollar, I'm still eatin' on the cheap. However, there definitely will not be any more rushing

through my food. I'll finally be able to sit and savour a delicious home cooked meal.
I'll be able to chew each morsel twenty-five times, ensuring full digestion, and still have time to consciously make sure it goes down the right tube.

* three meals per day
* times fifty forks per meal
* times thirty seconds per fork
* plus conversation . . . that would equate to:

Time for Eating	2.5 hours
Time Remaining	3,673.5 hours

Looking back at the big three — sleeping, exercising and eating — I am amazed at how many hours they absorb, even on Mercury. It actually doesn't leave me as much free time as I thought.

4. FAMILY TIME
Ideally this would include a movie AND a game. Assuming the movie is not *Lord of the Rings* . . . and I win the arm wrestling competition as quick as usual, I would have:

Time for Bonding	5.0 hours
Time Remaining	3,668.5 hours

5. HOUSE CLEANING
Forget fifteen minutes a room; I'm doing thirty!

Time for Cleaning	4.0 hours
Time Remaining	3,664.5 hours

After that, the rest is gravy, baby! Use it or lose it.

6. Twitter/Facebook

Socializing (mostly Farmville)	3,664.5 hours
Time Remaining	0.0 hours

And I still have time to watch *The Best of Kirsten Dunst.*
Now there's time well spent!
Applying for my Mercurian citizenship tomorrow.

He's Thankful; He's Thankful Not

I always celebrate Thanksgiving in October . . . and no, I'm not a month early. I'm Canadian.

There are many things to be thankful for . . . and some, not so much.

I am thankful for (in no particular order):

1. The Sun

   I'm not sure we need it anymore, because of electricity and all, but it's still pretty to look at.
2. Wire

   Without the wonder of wire, my wonky shelf unit would have collapsed, my car's muffler would be dragging along the road, and I would still have buck teeth.
3. Depends®

   Not having to stop every hour to pee certainly makes road trips a little more manageable . . . and quicker.
4. Digital Clocks

   Trying to figure out those clocks with the spinning sticks gives me a headache, especially the ones with Roman numerals . . . which not even the Romans use anymore.
5. Leave a Penny; Take a Penny

   Why would I leave one if I can take one? I don't know why stores are giving away pennies, but I've made a comfortable living taking a penny (or two) here and there.

6. Idiots
   My many encounters with them have led to the building of a solid comedy career.
   Keep up the good work, dimwits!
7. My Brain
   According to scientific studies, if I didn't have a brain I wouldn't be able to write a regular blog. I'm not sure of the reasons, but being brainless probably slows down your typing speed.
8. My Children
   Having little servants around the home makes life so much easier.
   "Hey, kid! Get Daddy another bon-bon."
9. Clothes
   I find clothes very restrictive and would rather go without. However, for some people, I feel the wearing of clothes is an absolute necessity, if only for my own peace of mind.
10. Girl Guide Cookies
    Those mint ones are the bomb!

On the other side of the coin, I am NOT thankful for (in no particular order):

1. Cheese Whiz
   I don't eat it . . . and I never will. I briefly considered it would be less of an issue if someone manned up and removed the word "cheese" from the title.
   Then I thought about it some more and realized that, regardless of name, its mere presence in our world simply creeps me out.

2. The Tooth Fairy

   A myth like this creates an air of cynicism that ultimately causes people to question reality.

   The lies regarding the Tooth Fairy (and the Easter Bunny, for that matter) have helped put Santa's existence on trial *. . . and that's ridiculous.*

   Don't doubt, kids, or Santa's sleigh won't work.

3. Earphones

   I can't tell you how many times I've shared some great story with someone only to have them end up staring blankly at me as they remove their earphones.

4. Cheese Whiz

   It deserves to have multiple mentions.

5. See No. 4

6. See No. 5

7. Ken

   This little plastic doll has done nothing but create an unhealthy body image for men. Not everyone has broad shoulders, a perfect tan, and wicked abs like Ken . . . and me. Why couldn't they have made him more universally realistic, like Barbie?

8. The Cadbury Secret

   It's the sole reason I have eternal bags under my eyes. Cadbury, how do you get the caramel in the bar? Just tell us already! It's driving me crazy.

9. Arms

   I am all for being able to hold and carry things, but I simply do not know what to do with these appendages at bedtime.

They would be on the "Thankful For" list if only someone could figure out how to make them detachable.

10. ELMO

    No one likes him. No one ever has. He's the poor man's Barney (who no one liked, either).

Confessions of a Sick Man

(as in ill, not deranged)

Sick and tired of being sick and tired. Enough already! Here is a detailed diary account of my last 24 hours (as of bedtime last night):

11:00 p.m.	Time for bed. Wanted to go earlier, but had a three-hour nap at 2:00 p.m., followed by a two-hour nap at 5:00 p.m.
11:37 p.m.	Still awake. Feeling chilled. Need more blankets.
12:00 a.m.	Have to go to the bathroom. I'm sure I went before bed, but I guess not.
12:48 a.m.	Opening new Kleenex® box. Took two Tylenol®.
1:00 a.m.	Still awake. Feeling really, really hot. Taking off blankets . . . and shirt.
1:03 a.m.	Sweating like a pig in heat. Taking off wool socks.
1:08 a.m.	Feeling chilled . . . again. Starting to think I'm going through menopause.
1:11 a.m.	Googling "menopause".
1:25 a.m.	Discovered it's not menopause.
1:32 a.m.	Going to the bathroom. Thought I went about an hour ago . . . guess not.
1:48 a.m.	Opening new Kleenex® box. Took two Tylenol®.
2:18 a.m.	Can't . . . breathe. Scraping crusties off my nose. Bad idea. Floodgates opened.

2:20 a.m.	Opening new Kleenex® box. Took two Tylenol®.
2:47 a.m.	Never realized how many of my neighbours are up at this hour.
3:17 a.m.	Still listening to my great neighbours.
3:37 a.m.	Wishing my great neighbours would *shut up!*
3:50 a.m.	Had a solid thirteen-minute sleep. Dreamed about being on a cloud. It was beautiful.
3:51 a.m.	Discovered I've fallen into my pile of used Kleenex®. *Ewww.*
4:23 a.m.	Stomach is upset. Spent the last twenty minutes staring into my toilet bowl. It's much cleaner than I thought it was.
4:25 a.m.	Oh well. Clean toilets are overrated.
4:36 a.m.	Opening new Kleenex® box. Took two Tylenol®.
5:00 a.m.	Still awake. Going downstairs to watch TV.
5:01 a.m.	Remembered I don't have a TV. Going back to bed.
5:12 a.m.	Feeling hungry. Going to have a bowl of Lucky Charms® for a snack.
5:17 a.m.	Went to the bathroom. Filled the bowl with Lucky Charms®.
5:26 a.m.	Pillow feels wet.
5:30 a.m.	Saying goodbye to Heidi as she leaves for work. Switching pillows.
6:47 a.m.	Enjoyed a solid seventy-seven minutes of sleep. Feel energized to start my day.
6:52 a.m.	Ready for a nap.
6:54 a.m.	Opening new Kleenex® box. Took two Tylenol®.
7:02 a.m.	Pillow feels wet.

7:30 a.m.	The sun is starting to shine through the window. Not good. I can now see why my pillow is wet. Hard to tell what is drool and what is nasal fluid.
7:31 a.m.	Flip pillow over.
8:00 a.m.	Eating a good hearty breakfast of eggs, bacon, sausage, and pancakes.
8:20 a.m.	Went to the bathroom. Decided it's best to just have toast . . . dry.
8:30 a.m.	Taking two Tylenol®.
9:00 a.m.	Began homeschool with the kids. Started math with my seven-year-old: "If Daddy can have two Tylenol® tablets every four hours, how many should he take in eight hours?" "Four," Connor answered. Yep. I was afraid of that.
9:10 a.m.	Assigned twelve-year-old daughter a research project on "how to pump a stomach". Due in one hour.

9:20 a.m.	Throat is really dry. Getting a drink of water.
9:22 a.m.	Going to the bathroom.
10:10 a.m.	Read my daughter's project. Thirty-six pages, with diagrams. Impressive, but she spelled Tylenol® with an "i". D-minus.
11:02 a.m.	Really need a Tylenol®. Don't want to risk it.
11:15 a.m.	Going for a walk to get some fresh air.
11:17 a.m.	Back home. Feeling wiped.
11:20 a.m.	Opening a new Kleenex® box.
11:23 a.m.	Found kids jumping in the cloud. Told them to stop.
11:24 a.m.	Went to the bathroom. Feeling a lot better.
12:00 p.m.	My oldest daughter made lunch. Eating with the kids.
12:20 p.m.	Went to the bathroom. Told daughter she gave me food poisoning.
12:25 p.m.	Told her I was joking.
1:00 p.m.	Can't figure out why Jade is still crying. I *said* I was joking.
1:05 p.m.	Explained to Heidi, on the phone, why Jade is upset. Promised Heidi I'd never do it again.
1:07 p.m.	Opened a new Kleenex® box. Took only one Tylenol®.
2:11 p.m.	Lying down for fifteen-minute nap.
5:11 p.m.	Woke up. Went to the bathroom.
5:13 p.m.	Taking a pass on dinner . . . well, maybe just a little.
5:17 p.m.	Going to the bathroom.
5:30 p.m.	Leaving to drive Jade to her youth group.

5:40 p.m.	Stuck in a traffic jam.
6:05 p.m.	Going to bathroom. Sadly, am still in traffic jam.
6:27 p.m.	Just finished a sneezing fit. Two new records: twenty-five consecutive sneezes and twenty-five near collisions.
6:36 p.m.	New sneezing fit. Out of Kleenex®. I guess that's what sleeves are for.
7:01 p.m.	Finally dropped Jade off. Heading to the local Tim Hortons to kill time while waiting for her.
7:05 p.m.	Arrived at Tim Hortons. Went to the bathroom.
7:10 p.m.	Saw myself in the bathroom mirror. Hair is all dishevelled; face is pale; lips are cracked; eyes are bloodshot. I look like that guy Edward from *Twilight*. Not well at all. Doesn't help that I've wet my pants and there is snot on my sweater. Hope they serve me.
7:25 p.m.	Still waiting to be served. Just me and the man with the whiskey stench and piece of chicken in his beard. At least, I think it's chicken.
7:35 p.m.	I'm pretty sure I was in line before that guy. Oh well, at least I'm going to be able to get my hot chocolate.
7:37 p.m.	Enjoying my hot chocolate.
7:38 p.m.	Going to the bathroom.
8:00 p.m.	Finished a nice chat with the guy who smells like whiskey. Confirmed that it is chicken.
9:00 p.m.	Woke up. Went to the bathroom.
9:10 p.m.	Picked up Jade. She refused to wipe my nose while I drive. Teenagers!

10:00 p.m.	Arrived home. Heidi asked why her pillow was wet. I blamed our son Connor. Is that wrong?
10:15 p.m.	Taking two Tylenol®.
10:16 pm	Opening new box of Kleenex®.
10:17 p.m.	Going to the bathroom.
11:00 p.m.	Still awake . . . Still in the bathroom.

The Days of Our Lives

If the cosmetic surgery explosion has taught me anything it is that everything could use a little updating now and then, and even ugly people have a chance.

With that first lesson in mind, I've been thinking it may be time to reconsider the days of the week. After all, and I'm no historian, naming them after gods and planets is definitely pre-80s. So, here is a fresh, much more relatable look at our week:

Monday: *"Moan" Day*

There isn't a person alive (or dead, for obvious reasons) who jumps out of bed on Monday morning with joy coursing through their veins. Those who do are quickly restrained by the mental health nurses assigned to watch over them.

Tuesday: *Make up for Monday Day*

Tuesday is a day of frenetic activity, with two days' work needing to be done in one . . . mainly because most people spent Monday moping, dragging their feet, and cursing its very existence.

Wednesday: *Phonics Appreciation Day*

Phonetically speaking, Wednesday is the perfect day to celebrate the best English language training tool since Dick and Jane ran. After all, how do you spell Wednesday? Just the way it sounds.

THURSDAY: *Five Stages of Grief Day*

1. Denial: "It's Friday!"
2. Anger/Blame: "*What*?! Stupid Thursday pretending to be Friday! I oughta . . ."
3. Bargaining: "Can I have tomorrow off?"
4. Depression: "Another day, another dollar . . . minus fifty percent in taxes."
5. Acceptance: "I might as well accomplish something. Anyone want to sit on the photocopier?"

FRIDAY: *The Lord's Day*

Most people believe that Sunday is "The Lord's Day". However, Friday should be the bearer of such a title because it is clearly the most spiritually unifying day of the entire week. Even the atheist thanks God for its arrival.

SATURDAY: *Half Day*

"Oh, it's 3:00 p.m. I guess I should get up . . . maybe just fifteen more minutes . . ."

SUNDAY: *Preparation Day*

Some people go to church. Some people watch football. But *everyone* is spiritually, emotionally, and mentally trying to prepare themselves for Moan Day.

NO CHARGE

There's a question I just have to ask. Who among you doesn't like free stuff?

Thank you . . . I see that hand.

Uh . . . actually, no I don't. Because *everybody* likes free stuff!

However, there are some people who honestly believe nothing in life is free. That's crazy.

I mean, did you know you can actually get *anything* you want for free? That's right. It's called stealing . . . but it's frowned upon.

So let's keep it real. Here's how I perceive life:

CLERK: Good morning, sir. Welcome to the Life Store.

DUDE: What's shakin', my man?

CLERK: Only the stomach of a belly dancer.

DUDE: Word up, bro.

[*Dude and Clerk exchange five-minute elaborate handshake to solidify their newly established brotherhood.*]

CLERK: So . . . what can I get you?

DUDE: I'm in need of some serious air.

CLERK: Well, we've got air ranging from your standard country to L.A. smog, but we're presently promoting Himalayan air, and we might still have some Chernobyl in the back room.

DUDE: Himalay . . . *what?*
CLERK: As clean as it gets.
DUDE: Done. Do you have any sunshine?
CLERK: Does a baboon have a red butt?
DUDE: The ones I've seen.
CLERK: One box of sunshine or two?
DUDE: Two please.
CLERK: Ah . . . heading on vacation, eh?
DUDE: Honeymoon, actually.
CLERK: Oooh. You're gonna need to get yourself some Love.
DUDE: All over that. Load me up with seven days' worth.
CLERK: I'll give you a lifetime's worth . . . and throw in a little Joy.
DUDE: Sweet!
CLERK: Indeed.
DUDE: So, what's the damage?
CLERK: Nothing.
DUDE: All that stuff is *free?*
CLERK: Would you like a receipt?

Some of the greatest things in life are a handout. Use them freely . . . you can always get more!

VOICE RECOGNITION ... OR NOT

Believe it or not, the same day I discovered an old-school typewriter, I was also made aware of my computer's voice recognition capabilities. Within six short hours, I went from wading in a ripple from the past to riding the wave of the future. That's quite a shift, and I could have really hurt myself—even more than I did when carrying that beast of a typewriter home.

I was really excited about this new-fangled technology. Not only did it have the potential for quick dictation, but it would be much easier on the wrists, not to mention the back. I mean, carrying a headset, instead of a typewriter, creates a lot less stress on the lumbar region (cool word, *lumbar*).

Now, if I understood correctly, voice recognition would allow me to sit and talk while the dream machine typed out my thoughts.

How awesome is that! And since I wasn't able to type my blog on the ancient typewriter, due to ribbon "dryness", I figured the next best idea was to go to the opposite extreme and do my whole blog the way NASA people do it.

With this state-of-the-art technology, how could my blog end up being anything but the best blog in the whole world? So, with Timmy at the helm, the great and mighty *S.S. Voice Recognition* set out on its maiden voyage.

How did it go? Well . . . just sit right back and you'll hear a tale, a tale of a fateful trip.

It was not pretty. It was a rough ride. It did not take long to realize that "voice recognition" would NOT be the wave of MY future.

What you are about to read is the actual transcript of my very first attempt at using voice recognition. No practice. I just set it up and started writing.

I've put the more coherent moments in italics, and the only editing was to break the dictation into paragraphs — or, at least, into what looked like paragraphs:

Timmy has entered the 21st century.

*This blog is being dictated using voice recognition.*You would think that it would be easier to Ste to type, but as you can see my stutter appeared.

This is one of the weirdest things I have ever experienced. I'm not sure if this egg knowledge you will help me or make the process longer.

As you can see, it didn't understand the word technology. Although, come to think of it, I think I'll refer to technology as "egg knowledge" from now one.

Oral on. Oral on? *What I meant to say was "or on".* Press paste.

Apparently saying "press space" is equivalent to saying "press paste".

Start Timmy♡ has entered the 21st century. *I'm not sure what that little heart sign is?*

Double space pressed double space. Double space I'm not so sure I'm going to dictate to enable logs. No that would be the logs not logs I said go to know no It[symbol] an old O. *I spend more time trying to correct* the knowledge.

Dole, dolls what Dole? Double space that pressed space pressed space.

The *The 21st century isn't really that convenient* the world's only go to articulate us at five you. If he'll understood that last sentence then maybe it will continue to dictate. *That really should read I will continue to dictate.*

I am not a big fan of voice recognition. It seems to recognize that I have a voice. It also seems to recognize most of the words that I speak. But I find that I'm speaking like a William Shatner one of the all expel William Shatner right. Although its belt no its spell to know. I said spelt to knott's belt too in knots belt at two.

This may not be the best example of how voice recognition should work, or be used for that matter.

I think that oak a cough is translated as that. But the word all which I just said is translated as all clear or all clear depending on what time I made to quote. I I am not the fastest type are in the world but neither is voice recognition.

I would be able to delete my misspelled words and rewrite them quicker than I am able to speak, then correct, and then re-speak in I would be where we - speak no not we dashed speak and we know that we dashed to speak to three at its three at a it's ex Clem Asian poinat.

End.

My final thoughts on voice recognition:

"Exclamation point" is translated "ex Clem Asian poinat."

Enough said.

The Twelve Wacky Days of Christmas

Even though *The Twelve Days of Christmas* was first published in 1780, it would be almost two centuries before the English language had a word to properly describe this legendary Christmas carol:

> *over-kill* (ō-vər-'kil) transitive verb
> To obliterate (a target) with more nuclear force than required.
>
> ~ Merriam-Websters Dictionary

I think it would be safe to say that generations of praise for the "True Love" in this poem has been slightly misguided. A closer look reveals an overly zealous suitor whose "Love Language" becomes painfully obvious when he obliterates the target of his affection with an excessively toxic display of gift-giving.

Let's take a moment and step into the shoes of the poor soul on the receiving end . . .

Day One ~

The True Love arrives.

"I come bearing gifts!"

"Oooh. I love gifts! What did you bring me?"

"Guess."

"Is it a sweater?"

"No."

"A movie?"

"No."

"Oh my goodness! It's a puppy! *You got me a puppy!*"

"Nope. Better!"

"Better than a puppy?"

"It's a partridge!"

"A what?"

"A partridge!"

"A partridge . . . ?"

"Yes! And—"

"A puppy!"

"No. A pear tree!"

Talk about disappointment, but then the True Love announces this is only the beginning.

Day Two ~

There is a knock at the door. It's the True Love, and he's hiding something behind his back.

"What do you have for me today?"

He quickly reveals his left hand.

"Is that a . . . turtledove?"

"Nope," says the True Love.

He reveals the other hand.

"It's two turtledoves!"

Silence.

"And . . ." he says.

"Oh, there's more?"

"Oh yeah, there's more. Another partridge!"

"Another . . . partridge?"

"And . . ."

"Yes!"

"Another pear tree."

It is so silent you could hear a jaw drop.

Day Three ~

Knock, knock.

There is the True Love, with a giant box. He teases by slowly lifting the lid. The excitement builds, inch by inch, until . . .

Ta-da!

"More birds?"

"Yep. Three of them."

"Hens?"

"French. And . . . two more turtledoves."

"Uh . . . thanks. I now have nine birds."

"Ten."

"Ten?"

The True Love reveals yet another partridge . . .

And another pear tree.

Day Four ~

HONK!

The True Love is in the driveway, motioning towards the trunk of his car.

"Do I hear chirping?"

Without responding, he pops the trunk.

"Are those *all* for me?"

"Sure are! Four calling birds, three French hens, two turtledoves, and—"

"A partridge."

"How'd you know?"

The True Love brings the birds into the house and then asks for help carrying the pear tree.

Day Five ~

Someone is at the door. I wonder who?

Yep. It's the True Love. This time he requests closed eyes and an outreached hand, which is reluctantly granted. After all, no one wants bird poop in their palm.

But a pleasant surprise it is. The True Love gently slides a gold ring on each of the extended fingers.

"*Gold!*"

"Yes, and . . ."

A truck pulls up in front of the house.

"More gold?"

"No. More birds! Four calling birds, three French hens, two turtledoves and—"

"I know, I know. A partridge."

"And a pear tree!"

"Of course."

Day Eight ~

A knock at the door.

"Who is it?"

"It's me, your true love."

"Hold on a sec. I just stepped on another goose egg."

"Where should I put the seven swans?"

"Out the back, with the ones from yesterday."

"What about the cows?"

"*Cows?*"

The True Love is standing in the midst of eight cows. He introduces the milkmaids (that came with the cows), hands over five gold rings, takes the swans to the pond, leads twenty-three other birds into the house, and plants another pear tree.

Day Twelve ~

It's been a really hectic couple of days. Along with the addition of more birds, cows, and milkmaids, there are now eleven pipers piping and forty-seven lords and ladies, leaping and dancing all over the place.

"Does anyone hear that? Please tell me that's not drums!"

Sure enough. The True Love is on the lawn, surrounded by twelve drummers, more pipers, dancers, maids, cows, and birds.

He holds up five more gold rings . . . and takes a big ol' goose egg off his head.

Within minutes, a police cruiser is added to the mix and the True Love is taken away.

There will be no Day Thirteen.

Grand total, including what's on the lawn:

* Forty cows;
* One hundred and forty noisy roommates;
* One hundred and eighty-four birds;
* More pears than stars; and . . .
* *Zero* True Loves.

What about the forty gold rings?

Sold.

How else would you be able to feed all those freeloaders?

Hey, January 17! Stick it Up Your . . .

While reading the paper this morning, I discovered that today is a very sad day. In fact, January 17 is *the* most depressing day of the year, and there is a mathematical formula to prove it.

I don't know what's more depressing: knowing that information or knowing someone took the time (and probably got paid) to figure that information out.

Now, I'm not sure what the formula is, but it probably takes into account the following realities:

By January 17 . . .

. . . every New Year Resolution has been broken;

. . . all credit cards are maxed; and

. . . all fridges are turkey-less.

I kind of wish I had picked up the newspaper earlier because until I read that article I had been in a really good mood. In fact, I gave props (New Year Resolution #3: *Use more street slang*) to the editor. I mean, if the paper had not made me aware of the situation, I might have gone through the most depressing day of the year all cheery-eyed and giggly. How embarrassing!

So, I turned my smile upside down and began sulking.

Three minutes later, I was bored and thirsty. I dragged my feet to the kitchen and, without lifting my head, reached into the cabinet. After mopingly swinging my hand around, I finally located a glass. However, my grip was so loose — what with my energy level being depressed and all — that the glass tumbled to the floor, shattering into a million tiny pieces . . . and one *really* big piece.

I sighed.

Emotionless, I swept the damage under the counter. Then, leaving a trail of blood, I dragged my sliced foot up to the bathroom to begin cleaning the wounds.

I rolled my eyes.

Picking glass out of your toes when you're depressed is slightly more difficult than I had imagined.

With a complete lack of focus and care, I plucked out the individual shards — starting with the easiest — and tossed them, one by one, into the garbage pail across the room.

Some made it. Some didn't.

Whatever.

I wanted to go downstairs again, because I was still thirsty, but it was way too far. So, I leaned over the bathroom sink, placed my mouth in the general vicinity of the faucet, and turned on the cold water.

Wrong tap.

Woe is me. My face is burning.

Two deep breaths later, and one slow (*really* slow) blink of despair, I gained enough emotional strength to pull my head out from under the scalding waterfall.

Curled up in the corner of the bathroom, lying in a puddle of something (and on a few glass chips that fell short), I began to reflect on life. Then it hit me!

There is still turkey in my fridge.

My credit card is paid off.

My New Year Resolution to remain a lifelong non-smoker is still intact!

This isn't a depressing day after all.

I leaped into the air, striking my *High School Musical* side-kick pose, bandaged my foot, iced my left cheek/jaw/ear, and hobbled downstairs to listen to ABBA.

Life *is* good . . .

Always!

Top Ten Reasons I'm on Social Media

Of all the questions I'm asked—or at least all those not related to my amazing abs—the one that seems to surface most is, "Why are you on social media?"

Now, depending on where the emphasis is added, that question can lead down many paths. For example, some inquirers emphasize the words "social media," as in: "Why are you on *social media* instead of, say, drugs?"

Others put the emphasis on "you," as in: "Why would *you*, a man with such great abs, need anything else?"

Still others stress the "why," as in: "*Why* do you feel it is important to have profiles on Twitter and Facebook?"

It is this final question I plan on answering today, with the top ten reasons I'm on social media:

1. If it's good enough for Grandma, it's good enough for me.
2. Talking to my kids = thirty minutes.
   Lurking on my kids = five minutes.
   A no-brainer.
3. Always only a click away from letting the world see my abs.
4. Without Facebook, I'd have no idea how many events I'm not invited to.
5. A paltry twenty-five friends simply doesn't cut it!
6. No one phones me anymore.

7. How else can the government keep tabs on me for my own safety?
8. I can't sleep if I don't know what everyone has had for lunch.
9. Twitter is how I met (it *will* happen) Alyssa Milano (see #3) and Ben Stiller.
10. I'm not. I have people do it for me.

Things I Will Never Say, Ever

(In a Million, Billion Years)

In her blog, *A Farm Wife*, my good friend Diane Loew once reflected on the things she never thought she would say. She had a very interesting list, and it inspired me.

You see, there are plenty of things I could write in that regard. The list of things I never thought I would say would probably start with:

"Can I try on those pink, arm-length, plastic gloves used to inseminate cows?"

Which, funnily enough, was said while in the company of Diane and her husband, "Farmer".

But I'd like to take her thought process one step further. Here is my list of things I will NEVER SAY, *EVER*, in a million, billion years:

1. *"Hey, let's go vote!"*

   Now, I'm not totally against voting, but I do feel democracy takes up too much time. It would be much easier if we all just voted for a dictator, and then sat back and let him rule as he sees fit . . . until he dies and the keys are handed over to whichever successor he didn't get around to murdering. Yeah, our taxes may go up, and we might lack the basic necessities of life (while our leader bathes in a gold tub), but at least we wouldn't have to walk over to the polls every four years. I've got better things to do.

2. *"Sure, you can bring your unicorn over."*
   Look, I love unicorns as much as the next guy, and I think it would be cool to have a friend who owned one, but I would never, under any circumstances, let that magical beast into my home. I mean, one wrong turn and that spiralled horn would gouge my wall so badly it would take thousands of dollars, or a sorcerer, to fix it. Quite frankly, I won't take that sort of financial risk . . . and there's no such thing as a sorcerer.
3. *"Hmm. Should I get the blue Speedo® . . . or the pink one?"*
   It's the hesitation that's key. Obviously, blue.
4. *"Thanks for entertaining at my party. Your clown makeup is awesome!"*
   First, there is simply no way I'd ever hire a clown because I have no desire to celebrate anything by having a stroke-inducing panic attack.
   Second, nobody in charge of throwing me a party would hire a clown because they would have no desire to celebrate anything by receiving a bloody nose.
   Third, clown makeup is NOT awesome. It's creepy at best, hellish at worst. Clowns are the most distressing form of entertainment this side of Barney.
5. *"Nuke 'em!"*
   Allow me to clarify. There have been many frustrating moments when I have screamed those words at the top of my lungs, to the horror of those around me. A certain Sunday morning church service comes to mind. And I will probably utter those very words again; however, I won't ever be able to passionately call down a radioactive

explosion on anyone while actually possessing the power to make it happen . . .

Unless, of course, the people choose me to be their dictator.

Y2K: A FAMILY SURVIVES

The time is 11:50 p.m. The date is December 31. The year is 1999.

We are ten minutes away from the total collapse of the world as we know it.

At the stroke of midnight, computers will explode, planes will fall from the sky, and nuclear missiles will launch. Total anarchy is just moments away.

In less than six hundred seconds, ATM machines will begin firing twenty-dollar bills onto the streets, security systems will be disabled, and left-in-the-dark governments will crumble.

The countdown to primitive life has officially begun.

At the dawn of the year 2000, a collective scream of horror will shake the very foundation of the earth, as billions of people awake to their VCR clocks flashing 12:00:00.

But don't expect the Boyles to face such peril.

The time is 11:50 p.m. The date is December 31. The year is 2009.

It has been exactly ten years since my family and I first settled into our remote, northern Manitoba bunker. I bet Mr. Y2K-is-a-bunch-of-malarkey wishes he'd listened to me now.

Loser.

From the moment I caught wind of the impending technological crash, I began the plans to build our little "ark", if you will. Not being much of a handyman, I had to spend hours sitting at the feet of the master — Bob Vila.

Surprisingly, he had taped no episodes about building bomb shelters, but apparently the combined knowledge I received about bathroom tiling, fixed mouldings, and using stucco, has served my family well. My little underground homestead has kept us safe all these years.

Bob, if you're alive . . . thanks.

Now, I will admit that it hasn't been a very comfortable decade, but no doubt it's been luxury compared to the carnage and chaos endured by those who didn't heed the Y2K warnings.

Assuming anyone has survived, at all.

I think the hardest part has been finding things to entertain us. This was a surprise because I really believed that was the area I had the best handle on. I mean, with our battery-powered TV, battery-powered VCR, and the entire second season of *Beverly Hills 90210*, we were going to be good for years. That crazy Brenda; she makes me laugh.

However, three hours after closing the bunker door, my wife informed me she had forgotten to pack the batteries. I was so mad!

So, every Thursday night for the last ten years, my family has acted out a *90210* episode (we celebrated our 500th performance a few months back). I always play Brenda. "What are we doing here? Just having milkshakes?" HA, HA! That Brenda; she makes me laugh.

We also had Twister®, but that game lost its appeal about two months in. It wasn't that the kids got bored playing as much as it was the fact we had also forgotten to bring deodorant.

I knew I should have made a list.

Now, although we've mainly been living off canned peas and water, the family seems to be doing rather well . . . that is, aside from everyone having lost a tremendous amount of weight . . .

and teeth . . .

and hair.

I'm not exactly sure what I look like because I forgot to bring a mirror, and catching your reflection in a dime just isn't the same. I keep telling my kids: "I look like the Queen!"

Apparently, that joke got old back in 2005 (which is around tally mark 1,600 on the wall).

It would be fair to say that losing weight has been a bit of a problem, seeing that all our clothes fit perfectly when we entered the bunker. But I'll take baggy clothes over chemical fallout and worldwide devastation any day.

The good news is that I finally fixed our urine filter. I would have had it fixed a lot earlier, but my wife's constant nagging was driving me crazy.

"We need to drink clean water!"

"I'm not drinking pee!"

Blah, blah, blah.

Look, let's be realistic. Five people living 24/7 in a 6'x 5'3" room, for ten years, is bound to cause some family friction, even if the room boasts an absolutely stunning stucco ceiling.

Sure, it's always dark (our last glowstick faded two years ago), and yes, it's always cold (our heater runs on batteries), but like I tell the kids every day, "At least we're alive . . . unlike your silly friends who decided to take the new millennium head-on!"

We may not be dwelling in Utopia, but it's not exactly the "God-forsaken death trap" the children are wont to call it, either.

This generation is so spoiled.

Well, it's been quite an interesting ten years. Only five more until the time-lock allows us to brave the new world. And believe me, when we step out . . . we'll be kings!

The Boyles: The family that outsmarted Y2K.

I can't wait.

A Singular Focus

The countdown has begun. It is 10:00 a.m., and I have one day to submit a unique entry to a writing contest. It's time to hunker down and focus . . . after some Wii Fit™.

11:00 a.m. Can't feel my toes. I think I pulled something in my glutes. Stupid yoga. Gotta go lie down.

12:00 p.m. Wow. An hour-long nap wasn't quite in my plan. Really need to start writing. Is that my stomach growling?

1:00 p.m. Mmmm. I love leftover spaghetti. If I win this contest, I'm going to credit my wife's amazing meat sauce. Nothing like a happy stomach to get the creative juices flowing.

2:00 p.m. Well, that sauce certainly got something flowing. Really should have asked how long it had been in the fridge. My stomach is still spinning. Gotta go lie down.

3:00 p.m.

4:00 p.m. *Seriously*. Does my alarm not work? Now I really need to get down to business!

5:00 p.m. Picked up an amazing alarm clock. Checking four stores was a little time-consuming, but I got a great deal. Naps won't ever steal my time again.

6:00 p.m. How do I get this thing to stop flashing 00:00? The instructions are written in every language, *except* English.

That reminds me. I've got some writing to do. Where's my pen?

7:00 p.m. Why is it you can never find a pen when you need one? I've turned the house upside down. No pen anywhere.

But I did find *Batman*. I've been wondering where that DVD went.

8:00 p.m.

9:00 p.m. That was awesome! Jack Nicholson's Joker has some classic lines:

"Never rub another man's rhubarb."

"Where does he get those wonderful toys?"

"The pen is truly mightier than the sword!"

Shoot! I forgot about the pen . . . and dinner.

10:00 p.m. There wasn't a fresh meal in the fridge. I think I must have tossed about twenty Tupperware® containers away.

I really should start labelling that stuff.

Off to McDonald's.

11:00 p.m. So much for "fast" food. There were so many people in line you'd think a Happy Meal® was the most amazing thing on the planet.

Gotta eat quick 'cause I've got some writing to do.

12:00 a.m. Had no idea I owned so many Happy Meal® toys. Garfield, Muppet Babies . . . and those cool

	Halloween pails. Digging through my basement was like going on a treasure hunt of cheap '80s memorabilia. These need to be seen.
1:00 a.m.	
2:00 a.m.	Completed my first display case, ever. Apparently the hammering woke my wife. When she asked, rather angrily, why I was still up, I told her, "Writing". I wasn't lying. Off to write.
3:00 a.m.	It's hard to concentrate so late at night . . . with such cool infomercials on TV. A blanket with sleeves! Ingenious. I'm inspired.
4:00 a.m.	
5:00 a.m.	
6:00 a.m.	
7:00 a.m.	
8:00 a.m.	
9:00 a.m.	I guess I was tired. Only one hour to go . . . and I've got nothing. A lesser man would feel nervous, but I embrace the challenge.
9:59 a.m.	*And* . . . submit! It's a masterpiece!

Oops

Everyone makes mistakes, but not every mistake is equal. Some errors can simply be laughed off, while others may leave eternal scars. One solely affects the individual, yet another may topple an entire nation. There are mistakes caused by ignorance and mistakes brought about by sheer stupidity.

Life is filled with twists and turns, and as a result, it is sometimes near impossible to determine the outcome of one's decisions. However, there are actions that most certainly hold a higher risk factor than others.

In those cases, if the odds go in your favour, the "thrill" may end up being worth it. But if those same odds play out as they should, the payoff could be devastating.

So why do people risk making mistakes? Why do people go where they shouldn't go? Do what they shouldn't do? Why do people feel the need to occasionally drop the safety net, toss aside common sense and tempt fate?

I've been asking myself those questions a lot over the last three days. Except I've made it very personal:

Why did I do it?

Three days ago, I was doing just fine and life was good. Now, I wouldn't call it exciting, but it was . . . good. I have a supportive wife and three fantastic children; I don't make a whole lot, but I have a job I love; and after years of showing diligence in my decision-making,

I am now respected as a man who rejects impulse and errs on the side of caution. In the eyes of others, I represent patience, maturity and wisdom.

Sadly, that will no longer be true.

It's going to be very difficult to recover that image when I'm found behind these bars. A fence of shame is what it is.

You see, three days ago, my wife and kids left for a week-long visit to Grandma's. I stayed home because I needed to "get some work done".

I should have gone. Even my mother-in-law's house is better than this.

Watching them drive away produced such a weird feeling. I can't remember the last time I was "alone". There has always been someone around to keep me honest. But now, with that close accountability stripped away, it was just me . . . and that urge.

An urge that, once acted upon, left me trapped, hungry, tired, lonely, and filled with regret.

But it's the waiting that's killing me. I don't want to be found confined here. It's humiliating.

I will admit, I had been haunted by the urge for some time. For so long I've had the suppressed desire to do something new, something crazy, something . . . unsafe. And it wasn't some random new, crazy, unsafe thing. No, I knew exactly what I wanted to do.

For years I'd wanted to try it . . . just once, but I had always been deathly afraid of the consequences.

For good reason, apparently.

The odds were stacked against me from the start. The "math" didn't add up, yet I figured getting caught simply wasn't going to happen. After all, it never happens to you.

I tried to get my work done, I really did, but within a few hours I found myself obsessing over this deep, ridiculous desire.

I kept telling myself, "You're a husband! Is this what a man of responsibility would do? You're a father! Is this the example you want to leave for your kids? You're a respected man of the community! *Don't do it.* It's not worth it."

I usually listen.

This time I chose not to.

So here I sit. Caged like a bird. A reputation about to be shattered . . . and for what? A brief thrill.

I've had a lot of time to think. I'm a changed man. I really don't know what the people in my life are going to say when they find out, but I hope they'll be filled with mercy.

What I do know is that, once freed, never again will I be so foolish as to stick my head where it doesn't belong . . .

In the staircase banister.

TIMMY VS. THE LAWNMOWER

It happened. "Oh, s***!" (I actually said, "Oh, skip," but writing it with stars instead of letters is a more effective opening line.)

There I was, sitting in the middle of a sporadically mowed lawn, staring at my recently shattered living room window (now situated directly above a once flourishing, flower bed) and wondering where it all went wrong.

Did I mention the bruised ribs?

My day started off like any other day . . . with a tingling numbness in my left arm.

Every morning, for as long as I can remember, the first few minutes after waking are crucial for determining the overall outlook for the day. If the tingling feeling is because my arm is asleep after being crushed under a pillow all night, the day looks great. However, if the sensation is because I'm experiencing a heart attack . . . well, the day will probably take a bad turn. I'm riding a good streak, at the moment.

So, after my brief self-diagnosis came back positive, I slammed my arm a few times against the wall to get the blood flowing and leapt out of bed with all the excitement of a child on Christmas.

I flung open the blinds, gathered the birds around as I sang one of my favourite Disney songs, and told the young boy passing on the street to go buy the prize turkey in the window. Short of North Korea deciding now was the time to end it all for everyone, what could go wrong?

Did I mention the lacerated neck?

Since making the shift from lifelong city dweller to country villager, I have learned some strange and wonderful things about our world.

1. When you breathe deeply, air is not supposed to burn your throat;
2. Unlike the moon landing, stars are not a government conspiracy. I see them every night; and
3. If everything shuts down at 5 p.m., you don't die.

While the adjustment to clean air, dark night skies, and a slower pace has been surprisingly easy, there has been one hurdle. At times, it seems like my neighbours mow their grass *every* four hours. Apparently, to these village people, a well-groomed lawn is next to godliness (and the YMCA).

Having not participated, even once, in this daily ritual, I began sensing a community shunning was just around the corner. In fact, I could physically feel the disapproving stares; stares which had become strong enough to pierce the thick forest growing on my lawn.

This was the day! I had an empty calendar, the weather was great, and once again, my arm had foretold good things ahead.

Did I mention the swollen black eye?

I pulled the lawnmower out of our landlord's shed.

Hmm? It was very different to the one I had last used, and this caused a sudden revelation . . .

I hadn't mowed a lawn in almost thirty years.

You see, when I was about ten I asked my father if I could help cut the grass.

I tried.

It was boring.

Since then, Dad has done all the landscaping.

Then, when I got married, I moved into a townhouse with a concrete back yard. Therefore, I haven't really touched a lawnmower . . . until today.

How do you start it?

Thank goodness for Google.

Search: "How to start a lawnmower."

Fill the gas tank. Done.

Push the bubble—no more than seven times . . . but no less than four times. Done.

Pull the cord. Nothing.

Pull it again. Nothing.

Harder. Nothing.

Harder! Nothing.

Lean in and pull it *HARDER*!!

I'd never felt my own knuckles slamming into my eye socket before . . . but the mower had started.

I thought my parallel-line cutting plan was doing pretty good until I looked back and saw monstrous strips of grass in between each of my routes. Although my lot was beginning to look like a corn field, the bigger problem was how to cut around the tree. With one hand I held a branch back, while the other hand mowed . . . until the mower got jammed on a root. Then I needed two hands.

That branch whipped back faster than a ninja trying to behead an enemy. It was a bloody mess, but my head—with one eye slowly shutting—was mostly still attached.

Not a quitter, despite feeling dizzy and having no depth perception, I continued on.

The slow blood loss was beginning to affect my ability to steer, and I went straight . . . into the garden.

The petunias didn't stand a chance against those whirling blades, but the large decorative fountain was more than a match. Colliding with that marble garden ornament caused such a jolt that my swollen eye opened long enough to see the carnage.

With the mower handle now deeply lodged in my ribs, and a jugular emptying faster than a camp site visited by a hungry bear, I was left with no choice but to pass out.

How long my face was buried in a pile of blood-soaked, mulched petunias, I do not know.

What I do know (now) is that a lawn mower isn't heavy enough to use as leverage when trying to get off the ground.

The mower flipped, dropping me to my butt and flinging a nice size stone through my living room window.

"Oh, s***!"

Then . . . a tingling numbness in my left arm.

A little late for an omen, don't you think?

It's been a few months now since I took my very first ambulance ride. I've recovered fully, my garden is prettier than ever, the window has been replaced, and the grass is . . . chest deep!

As I stand in the middle of my forsaken lawn, waving at my glaring neighbour, I'm finally ready, after hours of therapy, to get back on that horse . . .

After I find it.

I know it's out here somewhere.

I am confident today is the day I will conquer this lawn! I have an empty calendar, the weather is great, and once again, my arm has foretold good things ahead . . .

MY COLOURFUL NIGHT

I woke up this morning. That's the good news. It's always a great way to start any day. But, as excited as I was to be alive, I just couldn't get out of bed. I was freezing!

You see, at some point during the night, my toes decided they weren't going to spend any more time under the covers.

What were they thinking?!

For a minute, I actually thought they had completely disappeared because I couldn't feel them at all. But then I saw one. The big one. Sticking straight up and ice BLUE!

Bluer than a truck stop comedy show.

I woke up my wife. She was concerned, and for good reason, seeing as I don't normally call on her at 3:30 a.m. In a panic, she asked what was wrong.

When I told her that my toes were cold, well . . . let's just say she was not happy—and *not* about my toes. Apparently, blue toes aren't a good reason to wake her. From the sound of her voice, I had no doubt her face was beet RED!

Redder than Santa fleeing a flaming chimney.

Well, after getting a good talkin' to, I couldn't get back to sleep. So I decided to go downstairs for a little late night TV—but not without my slippers. I turned the bedroom light on to look for them, and my wife was *not* happy. So I turned the light off. The room was pitch-BLACK!

Blacker than deep space . . . at night.

I couldn't see my hand in front of my face.

Or, unfortunately, that cabinet in front of my blue toe (good thing it was numb).

Once downstairs, and with light, I sat down to see what was happening on the tube.

Having channel surfed for a good fifteen minutes without seeing one quality wave, I was about to give up and head back to bed.

But then — I saw it.

The "must-have" in kitchenware. The *ultimate* culinary tool! It could slice, dice, cook, freeze, clean itself, and keep things fresh . . . all for just three easy payments of $12.95.

Within seconds, the studio audience rushed the stage as the host gleefully handed out box after box.

Those people were so lucky! I was GREEN with envy!

Greener than a seasick leprechaun.

Knowing I was on a tight budget, lacking self-control, and feeling it wasn't the right time to ask my wife for permission, I quickly turned off the set.

Just then, I felt a sharp pain in my toe. Oh, good. The thawing had begun. It also meant I must have banged my toe on the bedroom cabinet harder than I thought.

I looked down, horrified. My throbbing toe was no longer blue, but rather a deep shade of PURPLE!

More purple than King Barney in his entire royal garb.

I hobbled up the stairs, slowly opened the bedroom door, swerved to avoid the cabinet, and quietly climbed back into bed. I was tired, cold, had a sore toe and a grumpy wife . . .

and had missed my opportunity for the best kitchen utensil this side of the Ginsu® Knife.

What a night!

I muttered a complaint to no one in particular and fell asleep. I don't remember exactly what I said, but I can guarantee it was colourful.

Nothing blasphemous . . . but *definitely* colourful.

Turn of the Century Social Networking

There wasn't time to blink. Within seconds, I was floored by the overwhelming potential of social networking. To reach the world . . . hit SEND.

Awesome!

Monday night, I finally finished our family's submission for the Great Wolf Lodge Video Contest. It had consumed most of the last two weeks, but we *really* want this prize. Great Wolf Lodge is our happy place, and the prize is a dream opportunity — four weekend vacations.

Think about it. That's like . . . four weekend vacations!

One of the criteria to get into round two is based on the total number of views our entry receives. In other words, how many people can I get to watch our video?

I don't know, but on Monday, around 10:00 p.m., I started to find out when I posted the video on Facebook . . .

At 10:06 p.m. I pushed . . . SEND.

And then it started.

Someone watched the video!

Then another.

And another.

And another.

I was floored.

Shouldn't these people be in bed?

By 11:39, four of my friends had re-posted the video on their sites, and it had been seen thirty-six times. One hour and thirty-three minutes. Thirty-six views. That's a viewing every two and a half minutes.

Outstanding!

Now, I'm not trying to make it sound like amassing thirty-six views is the equivalent of landing on the moon (which we probably haven't done yet, if you look at the Internet pictures), but it was certainly a solid look into the potential of social networking. All I did was push "send" (or "share", for the Facebook geeks who take their Facebooking lingo seriously), and . . . *voilá!* Seventy-one views by morning.

Seventy-one views.

Overnight.

Astounding!

Imagine what would have happened if I had more than four Facebook friends. I should really think about adding some more people, but that's another article for another day.

It got me thinking. What would have happened if I had tried to get seventy-one people to see my Great Wolf Lodge video one hundred years ago? Oh the trouble I would have had . . .

August 24, 1912.

I gather my family of five together to pen seventy-one individual letters. Starting around 10:00 p.m., writing by candlelight with quill and ink, I figure we will be done around 12:30 a.m. Assuming, of course, there are no ink spills, kids fighting, or problems with the coyote that has been lurking around our sheep pen.

Then, giving the kids a break, I spend the rest of the night alone, loading up the horses for what will no doubt be a long ride.

At sunrise, with only three weeks' worth of water and grain, the kids and I mount up and head out, travelling the countryside, dropping our letters off at each of our friends' homesteads . . . which wouldn't be so bad if the stupid Miller family hadn't moved to higher ground because of the flooding.

"We want our kids to live in a safer neighbourhood," they said. Blah, blah, blah.

But we need them to see our video, so we press on, battling scurvy and losing a kid to the black plague on the way.

Due to the immense heat, five nasty confrontations with rattlers, and one of the horses breaking a fetlock, three weeks turned into two months . . . which, after the runaway-stagecoach incident, eventually became ninety-seven days.

Finally, having delivered our seventy letters (we never made it to the Miller's), we arrive home only to find our house burnt to the ground by those pesky Vikings.

Luckily, my wife was safe, as she had been hiding under the haystack where we keep the key to our barn. I told her no one *ever* thinks of looking there. . .

Then, after ALL that, we would STILL have to wait to see if anyone watched the video.

Ridiculous!

I guess videos made a hundred years ago simply weren't intended for mass consumption.

Want to see Timmy's Great Wolf Lodge video? Check it out on YouTube http://bit.ly/14Dj4ZT

YELLOW
A POETIC BUFFET

I have decided to write about some of the wonderfully yellow things in our world, but in a very un-yellow manner. You see, yellow is associated with cowardice, but I have chosen to bravely step out of my comfort zone and into an arena for which I am far from trained.

The arena of poetry.

Having just learned most of these poetic forms (within the last few hours), I present to you, without further ado (a fitting rhyme, to be sure):

A Few of My Favourite Yellow Things
(Ten Poems in Ten Styles)

Rubber Duck
(an Ode)

It is more beautiful than a rainbow.
It is even more precious than a rare gem.
More pure than water and fresh fallen snow.
More needed than legs, or eyes, or brain stem.
It is more refreshing than a cool rain.
Desired more than beauty or wisdom.
More powerful than a dump truck.
Worth more than gold and sleeker than a train.

And tastier than strawberry lip balm.
There is nothing compares to my old rubber duck.

Hannah Montana's Hair

(a Haiku)

Hannah Montana
She has those flowing blond locks
What? It's just a wig!

Lemonade

(a Ghazal)

Lemonade as sweet as thee.
You are much better than stupid iced tea.

Bananas

(an Acrostic)

Bananas are good.
Apples are not.
Neither are oranges,
Apricots,
Nectarines or
Antelopes.

Big Bird

(a Pantoum)

Big Bird is massive!
Big Bird is, by far, the biggest bird I've ever seen.
There is no bird like Big Bird.
I wouldn't want to clean Big Bird's cage.

Big Bird is, by far, the biggest bird I've ever seen.
I don't think Big Bird would make a very good pet.
I wouldn't want to clean Big Bird's cage.
The mess would be crazy!
I don't think Big Bird would make a good pet.
Big Bird is just too . . . big.
The mess would be crazy!
I think Big Bird would be too much to handle.
Big Bird is just too . . . big.
There is no bird like Big Bird.
I think Big Bird would be too much to handle.
Big Bird is massive!

Bumble Bee

(a Cinquain)

Yellow
Strong warrior
Transforming, protecting
An autobot above reproach
Beetle

Hulk Hogan When He Wore Yellow in the '80s

(a Sijo)

He comes to the ring, pointing to the
crowd like he can't hear them.
In moments, he is out cold, but you
can't stop the Hulkster!
Shaking his arm, he rises up to leg
drop his stunned opponent.

Sponge Bob

(a Limerick)

There once was a sponge with square pants,
Who wanted to learn how to dance.
His best friend was a star,
Who was very bizarre;
You can see how they didn't have much chance.

Smiley Face

(a Ruba'i)

It's a mind-boggling thought
That I've pondered a lot
Who knew that the key to happiness
Would be a big yellow dot!

The Sun

(*in a made-up style I have dubbed, "Poetic Licence"*)

Without the sun,
there would be none.
No light.
No heat.
No day.
Where would we stay
without its ray?
The dark.
The cold.
The night.
Oh no . . . may it never be so.
No heat strokes.

No sunburns.
No melanoma.
Hmmm.
A dark, cold night wouldn't be that bad, after all.

Having released my inner poet, I have come to realize it is not what you say or how you say it that matters, but rather, what you call it.

Some people will read anything if it's called poetry.

My Golf Day

(One Hundred and nineteen shots — Three Dead, Two Wounded)

People think golf is complicated, but nothing could be further from the truth. Just take a look at this dictionary definition:

Golf, *n.*

"a game in which a player using special clubs attempts to sink a ball with as few strokes as possible into each of the 9 or 18 successive holes on a course."

~ Merriam-Webster Dictionary

It's as simple as that, folks. Just use your special clubs to sink the ball into some holes.

What a relaxing game this "golf" must be.

I haven't golfed in over ten years . . .

Well, that's not completely true. The last decade has seen me conquer many a golf course using my special club to skilfully navigate balls up ramps, through windmills, and around revolving Smurfs. I even aced a hole, which probably caused lesser men to weep, by driving a ball deep into the mouth of a whale, out its spout, down its tail, and over the trailing dolphin. It was magical . . . if not heroic.

However, although these experiences fit the definition of golf to a tee (pause to laugh at this *very* intended pun), most "golfers" don't consider courses like Wally's Whimsical Putt-Putt Forest actual golf.

Whatever.

Anyway, I recently went to Trillium Wood Golf Course — a large, beautiful golf course with a surprisingly high level of difficulty . . . despite not having a single swinging monkey to dodge or any six-foot lollipops to weave your ball through.

Just a few hours before tee off, I unearthed my "big boy" golf bag from the basement. Needless to say, after a decade of inactivity, my clubs looked . . . out of shape.

Here are some very revealing details about my bag and the ancient relics it contained:

* There are eight "special" clubs, which includes two putters and two three-woods . . . so, technically, there are only six. Not exactly a full deck.
* The woods are *actually* made of wood. An outdated fire hazard for sure.
* My "set" consists of four different club manufacturers. I'm waiting for an official sponsor.
* I have a six-iron which I thought was a nine-iron. They shouldn't make six-irons. It's confusing.
* There is a fat putter and a skinny putter . . . which, quite possibly, was stolen from Wally's Whimsical Putt-Putt Forest.
* The ever-present rust on the telescoping ball-retriever shows it took a dip or two in the past.
* The dust bunnies were as big as golf balls . . . and numbered more than my last recorded golf score (one hundred and twenty-nine—June 3, 1997).

When the time came to unzip the side pocket of this golf-bag-shaped time capsule, I thought about recording an hour long video special leading up to the grand discovery, but then I remembered Geraldo Rivera and Al Capone's vault. Hence, no video.

I just opened it.

The verdict: I should have filmed it. I was clearly more successful than Rivera.

One dollar and seven cents, my friends! And . . .

* a glove forever molded into a withered arthritic hand;
* a toxic hand cloth;
* tips about how to golf (which I appreciate, but don't need); and
* a handful of those useless stubby pencils that even kindergarten teachers would throw out for being too short.

However, my favourite find was the head of a three-iron, which was (surprise, surprise) manufactured by a completely different company than all my other clubs.

Where the shaft is will remain a mystery, but most likely it was broken off after connecting with a tree, either on the follow-through of an epic shot made out of the bush or after being whipped down the fairway in a fit of immature rage because I was losing.

I lean towards the first scenario . . . but we'll never know.

Okay . . . so how did the day go? I'd describe my shots, in honour of the Scottish, as being a little off "kilt-er". I left three dead and two seriously wounded, but using only my seven, nine (or six), and the fat putter, scored a one hundred and nineteen.

I was ecstatic!

Sure, I'll admit the death toll and final tally were both way over par . . . but they were also lower than my previous golf experiences.

According to memory, I used to average one hundred and twenty-five, which was confirmed by the old score cards I found, proving my memory to be sharper than my golf game.

The lesson: Don't play golf . . . and you'll get better!

You see, after ten years of golf exile, I knocked six shots off my typical round. Therefore, if I don't play golf for another eighty years, I'll be awesome!

I've booked my next tee time for my one hundred and twentieth birthday. I'll shoot sixty-nine . . . and retire from the game.

What am I Thinking?

Psychics are a very interesting case study and, in general, they don't get a whole lot of attention — for good reason. They often look goofy and don't really bring much to the le, aside from the occasional catch phrase.

k about it. Does Batman *really* need Robin?

ly not! Holy Loser, Batman! Those movies went ST as soon as they added him. Robin is the le of a useless psychic.

at's "side kick". What was I thinking?

if you know the answer to that question then that *you* are the topic for today.

go I received a flyer on my car window. I hate it. F andering the parking lot, littering on my car. I don your flyers at home, why would I want them hen I' at home?

If I h get out of my car, after driving a few metres, to pull ur just noticed, flapping pamphlet from my windshield wiper, the chance of me happily embracing your information is pretty much zero. And believe me, if your flyer is promoting your amazing psychic powers, then it's DEFINITELY zero. I mean really, who wants a psychic who doesn't know putting their flyer on my car will irritate me? Isn't that their job?

To know stuff?

Apparently, according to the flyer I received the other day, the "most powerful" psychic in Europe has come to ply her trade in Canada.

Now, that got me thinking. If I were the "most powerful" of anything in North America, I'm not sure I'd pack up the tent and go anywhere else. I mean, that's a pretty sweet position to be in. What if I left home only to find out I was actually the second most powerful (or worse) in my new place of residence? How depressing.

So why leave?

Maybe she was tired of always being in the spotlight, not able to look at her own palm without the European paparazzi jumping all over her. Maybe the second most powerful psychic in Europe was arranging a coup, and she needed to escape.

Or maybe she thinks Canada's most powerful psychic is even faker than she is, leaving the door wide open for her to claim the title of "most powerful psychic in Europe AND North America". Wouldn't that look good on a business card?

Now, I really don't want to compare this person with other psychics and false prophets . . . mainly because her flyer tells me not to, sort of. Actually, it says not to compare her with "other psychics and false profits". It's too bad her "superior powers" package didn't include spell check.

Of course, she may also have a superior wit and be simply enjoying a little word play. She may actually have meant financial profits. While other psychics live on shoestring budgets, just pretending to live large, she makes a TRUE profit. Hey, if you want a session with the "most powerful", you've got to pay accordingly. She ain't giving it away.

Some time ago, I saw a large sign promoting a Psychic Fair, and I remember thinking that these people must be legit. I mean, the sign didn't have some general fortune cookie comment. It read: June 20th from 1:00 - 6:00 p.m.

Amazing!

These people knew EXACTLY when the fair was going to start AND end. If that's not foretelling power, I don't know what is.

But before making any real judgements on the psychic phenomenon, I figured I really should do some personal investigation. I'm aware of one particular psychic (not sure where she ranks on the most powerful scale) who offers one free answer to any question. I decided to take her up on the offer.

I sat down across from her and asked, "What's my second question?"

She didn't know.

I left.

Case closed.

Purple
A Colourful Conversation

Do you know what annoys me? Questions like that. I mean, really, how am I (or you, in this case) supposed to know the answer to that?

So, do you WANT to know what annoys me?

People who ask questions like that in written documents.

For goodness sake, we're not texting each other. It's not like I'm going to wait for you to respond before I continue.

So, here is what really annoys me — whether you do know, want to know, both or neither.

The colour purple.

Purple drives me crazy. It has such an attitude problem.

Recently, I had a chance to sit down with Purple, and the discussion was . . . well . . . colourful. The following is the transcript from that meeting:

Timmy: Purple, thanks so much for joining me today.

Purple: It is your pleasure.

Timmy: Pardon me?

Purple: You are pardoned.

Timmy: Um . . . I'm not sure about this, but it does seem that you are speaking down to me. I certainly apologize if I've misread your tone.

Purple: Oh, it is I who should be sorry. I meant to make it much more obvious.

TIMMY: So you *are* talking down to me?
PURPLE: You are surprised?
TIMMY: A little.
PURPLE: I am Purple.
TIMMY: Yes, I see that.
PURPLE: I am the colour of royalty.
TIMMY: Are you serious?
PURPLE: I am as serious as you are slow.
TIMMY: Hey, wait a second!
PURPLE: Commoner.
TIMMY: Whoa . . . now listen here, Mr. Last Colour on the Rainbow—
PURPLE: That is Violet. I am Purple.
TIMMY: Really? So you couldn't even make the rainbow.
PURPLE: I do not need to defend—
TIMMY: So, you're not a primary colour . . . or even a secondary colour. You, my friend, are nothing but a third-rate—
PURPLE: *I AM ROYALTY*!
TIMMY: Oh, you're royal all right. A royal pain in my—
PURPLE: I will not stand for this!
TIMMY: Look, you haven't been the colour of royalty since all inks and dyes became affordable to everyone.
PURPLE: I am a colour without *any* equal! I cannot be rhymed.
TIMMY: Neither can Orange.
PURPLE: *No*! This just cannot be! Orange is the colour of criminals.

Timmy:	And hall monitors.
Purple:	I will *not* be humiliated like this!
Timmy:	Purple Nurple.
Purple:	We're done here.
Timmy:	Oh, you were done a while ago.
Purple:	Good night!
Timmy:	Tell Violet I said "Hi".
	(Purple is *such* a maroon.)

Talking Without Typing—What a Novel Idea

Conversation is good. On Monday, I posted to Facebook, sent a direct message on Twitter, and even chatted on Yahoo. However, when no one responded, I eventually went to the stairs and yelled up to the kids to get off Facebook, Twitter and Chat and come down for dinner.

It was a great dinner. We texted some very funny jokes to one another.

Yesterday morning, I had a deeply intimate conversation with my wife. She told me she loved me, and I responded accordingly. Never mind that it was thirty-five minutes later, on her Facebook wall, while sitting in the same room.

It wasn't long before that particular post was flooded with so many comments I needed to scroll down twice in order to read them all. There were lots of "ah, that's sweet", and one "I love you, too" (which was written by someone taking a stab at humour . . . and missing horribly).

If my message had simply been "I love you", the would-be "joke" comment would have been no worse than clichéd. But my message *specifically* stated: "I love you, *Heidi*". The commenter's name was Jim. So that was just moronic.

Anyway, the other comment which sparked my interest was written by my good friend Steve. Of course, if it hadn't been for his dreadful spelling I may never have noticed it.

Steve's comment (after some decoding) read: "*When was the last time you had a conversation . . . face to face?*"

Hmm . . . face to face? Interesting. I didn't think people still did that.

It sounded like fun, so I decided to give it a try. After clicking "like" on his comment, I left the following response: "*Steve, I'll tell you . . . over lunch. Jim, you're a moron.*"

I was giddy. I was actually going to have a conversation—face to face.

Was I dreaming? Had I been transported back to the '80s? If it wasn't real, I was hoping for the latter, but would accept the former.

I left a voice message on my wife's cell phone informing her of the adventure I was embarking upon, and then ran out the door. I was so excited I forgot to tell her to check her phone message as I bolted past.

Arriving at the restaurant early, I had time to think—too much time. Realizing I wasn't quite sure what to say in a conversation—face to face—I began to sweat profusely. As a result, my iPhone slipped out of my hand and crashed to the floor.

The screen went blank.

I was alone.

My mind filled with questions faster than my email box fills with stupid joke forwards.

What do I do if I say something sarcastic? I won't have colon-bracket as my safety net.

What if Steve says something funny? Do I say LOL or ROFL?

How do I know when my sentence has reached its character limit?

How many characters can I use?

I was terrified.

Feeling a hand on my shoulder, I spun around to see Steve smiling at me.

"Hi," he said.

"Hey, Steve," I said.

Hmm. That wasn't so hard.

It was a great lunch.

Steve and I had an incredibly relaxing conversation—face to face. We laughed out loud, smiled for real, and didn't even count our words. It was exhilarating. In fact, we're doing it again next week . . . and inviting Jim.

I can't wait to tell everyone on Facebook.

An Inside Look at Writer's Block

A few hours ago . . . okay, many hours ago, I sat down on this very couch and rested my laptop computer conveniently on my . . . lap. I was preparing to unleash a flurry of words, which would soon form themselves into yet another insightful blog entry.

I couldn't help but think how much this next entry was going to dramatically improve the lives of those who would read it. As a result, my pulse rose to a feverish rate and tears of joy welled up in my eyes.

And then it happened.

Actually, "it" would be better described as "nothing", because *nothing* happened. Here I was with a heart ready to pour out love, and fingers ready to type out wisdom, but something wasn't right. Something was missing, and I just couldn't figure out what *it* was. Which isn't surprising because the something that was missing was my brain.

Heart and Fingers were primed and waiting, but Brain was nowhere to be found.

After an intense search, Brain was eventually discovered, curled up in the fetal position, fast asleep. Brain's waves were as flat as the voice of an eliminated *American Idol* contestant.

Heart screamed and yelled for Brain to wake up, but the emotional appeals fell on deaf ears. Now, I know Brain is not hearing impaired, so I figured he was either wearing earplugs or inside the Cone of Silence.

Fingers tried poking, prodding and nudging Brain, but even that couldn't bring about the slightest twitch.

Thinking Brain was dead, Fingers panicked and began shaking Brain mercilessly, to no avail.

Brain just mumbled something about Alyssa Milano and rolled over.

At least he was alive.

For countless hours, Heart and Fingers worked at stirring Brain. Heart even marched around banging cymbals and drums, while Fingers resorted to splashing Brain with water. However, it was becoming very clear that Brain had, simply, reached his limit. He was not going to wake up until he was full recharged.

For whatever reason, Brain was done.

With this reality before them, Heart and Fingers decided they would soldier on and complete the task without their good friend. But despite their good intentions, all they could muster was this:

:)

You see, without Brain guiding, Fingers simply couldn't put the cries of Heart into anything intelligible.

Brain ended up sleeping for what seemed like an eternity, only longer, but eventually Brain's waves did resume waving.

Sadly, by then, it was too late. Brain was now pumped and energized, but so much time had passed that Heart was now completely drained and Fingers was painfully locked in the textbook typing position. There would be no blogging today.

Writer's block. It's a simple reality of every writer's life, and it was bound to happen to me at some point.

I've just sat for hours in front of my computer, with nothing to show for it but watery eyes from the hypnotizing glow of my computer screen, and white knuckles. In fact, my hands moved so little that I think the letters ASDF and JKL: will be forever imprinted on my fingertips.

Wait a minute!

I just wrote this article.

Huh. How 'bout that?

Good save, Brain. Welcome back.

Writer's block? Whatever!

A Revolutionary Idea

It has become clear to me that online chatting has taken a prominent place in the lives of many. As a result, I have felt the need to pull up my socks and throw my hat into the world of internet communication.

Join them or be joined, as they say.

Over the last six months, I have poured my heart and soul into trying to discover a practical, down-to-earth way to enhance the cyberspace conversational experience for the masses.

Having left no stone unturned, and no chicken uncooped, I stand absolutely amazed (although creatively drained) at the gift I now have to offer the world.

Everyone (except the slower ones among us) knows that it is often difficult to explain yourself properly in a text message. Without the non-verbal cues people give in face-to-face conversation, even the most well-meaning comments often lead to confusion.

But no more!

Texters, Facebookites, Twits . . . this is for you. And I guarantee your world will never be the same again!

Using the symbols on any computer keyboard, I have compiled a list of characters that will change the face :) of cyber-dialogue — even more than emoticons.

I call them . . . punctuaticons:

1. Period .
2. Comma ,
3. Exclamation Point !
4. Question Mark ?

Use them.
No, seriously. *Please*, USE THEM!

My Great Wolf Day

The following is my moment by moment account of yet another family vacation at our favourite indoor waterpark resort:

11:30 a.m. Heading to the Niagara Falls Great Wolf Lodge for visit number thirteen.

12:55 p.m. Making the final turn. I can see it. It's beautiful!

12:56 p.m. Pulling over. Discovered I can't drive and cry at the same time.

12:59 p.m. Still feeling weepy with joy, but definitely able to recommence driving.

1:02 p.m. Going to get a luggage cart while the family stays to unpack the car.

1:03 p.m. Am I the only one skipping across the parking lot? Very odd.

1:04 p.m. Greeted by a wolf howl as I enter the main doors. I return the gesture.

1:05 p.m. Apologize for howling into the ear of an elderly lady. Honestly, I didn't see her there.

1:07 p.m. Found the luggage cart. Doorman wouldn't give me a ride on it. No tip.

1:12 p.m. Waiting in line.

1:14 p.m. After three attempts, finally got the wave going. To the end of the line and back.

1:17 p.m. Checking in.
1:22 p.m. The front desk employee asks if I've been here before. I ask if he is new.
1:25 p.m. Putting on my wristband. It's blue. A *gorgeous* blue.
1:28 p.m. Discovered I can't put on a wristband and cry at the same time.
1:32 p.m. Wristband is on. Hand is blue. I always make them too tight.
1:36 p.m. Exchanging wristband.
1:42 p.m. Heading to my room, paddling my cart like a surfer.
1:52 p.m. Ran over three kids (maybe four).
The parents blamed me. I blame the wobbly wheels.
1:53 p.m. Making a game plan.
1:58 p.m. Heading to the water park. Very excited for the debut of my Great Wolf Speedo®.
2:09 p.m. Commencing one-hour waterslide bonanza.
3:11 p.m. Fifteen slide runs. Three Speedo® compliments. One queasy stomach.
3:14 p.m. Entering hot tub.
3:18 p.m. Exiting hot tub. I don't care what that lady says. It *wasn't* me.
3:22 p.m. Entering wave pool.
3:27 p.m. Wow! Those waves were mighty strong.
Where's my Speedo®?
3:47 p.m. Still in the wave pool.
Still have no idea where that Speedo® went.

3:59 p.m.	Finally! Lifeguard told me someone had found it floating in the shallow end. When I asked why it took so long, he said they had to rule out all the kids first.
4:03 p.m.	Entering the lazy river.
4:48 p.m.	Woke up.
5:00 p.m.	Drying off and heading to the Arcade.
5:10 p.m.	Hitting the child casino with fifty tokens in my pocket. Daddy needs a new house!
5:13 p.m.	Cashing in my tickets: One stuffed banana. One cherry sucker. One Hannah Montana sticker. No house.
5:18 p.m.	Heading to Mini-Golf.

5:30 p.m. After four holes, I'm on track for my all-time lowest score, and I've only used three mulligans . . . and lost two balls.

5:36 p.m. Off the tree. Off the bench. Off the spinning wolf. Off the kid's head. Nothing but hole.

5:38 p.m. Staff member just took away my driver. Also suggested I should put some pants on. Not a fan of the Speedo®, apparently.

6:12 p.m. Finished with one hundred and twenty-two and a score card that's fit to be framed!

6:14 p.m. Time for dinner. I can't believe I've done so much and still have the entire evening AND all of tomorrow. This place is awesome! I think I'm going to cry.

Hey . . . where's my family?

6:15 p.m. Heading to the parking lot . . . with the luggage cart.

Back to School: A Big Bust

This morning I thought the world had come to an end. In the middle of an amazing dream about Ryan Seacrest and some dolphins, I was startled by a sound I would not wish upon my dearest of enemies.

Words cannot describe it . . . but if they could, I would say that it sounded like the primal scream of thousands upon thousands of tortured souls. It was absolutely deafening and so terrifying that it sent ice-cold shivers down my spine — not once, but twice . . . and a half.

Within seconds, a rumble of epic proportions, both in magnitude and longevity, shook my house so hard that my Alyssa Milano shrine came crashing to the ground.

Then there was a rush of wind, followed by . . .

Silence.

Well, except for the celebratory dance by my wife (who really never appreciated the shrine).

After stepping cautiously around my spinning wife (lest I got an elbow in the face), and climbing over the now half-bust of Alyssa (note that by "bust," I am referring to a sculpted head . . . at least in this case), I leapt to the window and ripped open the curtains.

I had expected to see that the sun had vanished from the sky and my neighbourhood had become a wasteland, but I was wrong . . . and, surprisingly, a little disappointed. Everything looked normal. It was just quiet. Really, really quiet. Then it hit me.

It's "Back to School" day!

That ungodly sound was actually the collective wailing of school-bound children.

The rumble was a result of countless families taking to the streets at the exact same time, trying desperately not to be late on the first day back (something of which many failed.)

The wind was nothing but one giant "sigh" of relief from parents everywhere.

As I stood staring out the window, I couldn't help but reflect on my own school days and amazing "first day" experiences.

Let's see . . .

* First Day Kindergarten — leaving Mom for the very first time. I cried.
* First Day Grade One — leaving Mom for the two hundred and twenty-seventh time. I cried.
* First Day Grade Two — bowl cut. I cried.
* First Day Grade Three — I'm wearing a handmade sailor outfit (gift from an aunt). I cried.
* First Day Grade Four — still reading at Grade Two level. I cried.
* First Day Grade Five — thought I was going to have to try smoking. I cried.
* First Day Grade Six — sporting a "fashionable" bowl cut. I cried.
* First Day Grade Seven — thought I was going to get beat up. I cried.

* First Day Grade Eight — I *knew* I was going to get beat up. I cried.
* First Day Grade Nine — I thought I was going to get beat up. I cried.
* First Day Grade Ten — wearing a handmade sailor outfit (same aunt). I cried.
* First Day Grade Eleven — I've finally moved on to Grade Three reading. Pretty excited.
* First Day Grade Twelve — accidentally slept in . . . I skipped.
* First Day Grade Thirteen — I slept in . . . on purpose. I skipped.
* First Day Year One College — thought I was going to have to do drugs. I cried.
* First Day Year Two College — *hmm*, can't remember. Did I *even* get to Year Two?

Oh, how I *loved* "Back to School" day.

Good luck, kids!

* First Day 2013 — Alyssa Milano bust broken. I cried.

Super-Dumb-stitions

Today is Friday the 13th (cue spooky music). It's going to be a busy day because my "to do" list is longer than a William Shatner monologue.

I am about to head out for a walk, but first I have to clean up the glass from the mirror I just broke.

I've decided to take Podgy, my black cat, with me for company.

Our first stop will be the grocery store, where I have to pick up a large bag of salt. After that, it's off to a nearby construction site to see how many ladders I can walk under.

On the way, I'll have to multitask, stepping on every crack possible while spilling the salt.

When I arrive home, I'll proceed to cut my nails, which according to some, is not a good idea on a Friday. But hey, living on the edge is what I do.

I will then sit back down to finish this article . . . and wait. Wait for the onslaught of calamity that I will have apparently brought upon myself during my activities.

If you're reading this article, it means I survived yet another brush with death.

Now, obviously, I'm not a superstitious person or I would not have even attempted to write this today. Starting a new task on a Friday is also supposed to be a bad omen.

I find superstitions amusing, and I think one of the quirkiest ones is fear of the number thirteen.

To me, it is very funny that some hotels still won't acknowledge the thirteenth floor. Is it their way of trying to send a message that superstitious people are welcome there? Actually, the opposite is true. When they re-number floor thirteen as floor fourteen, they are really saying, "We don't think superstitious people can do math."

Anyway, out of curiosity (which killed the cat, but not me) I spent some time looking into other obscure superstitions that have been (and still are) floating around in our crazy world.

Here are my thoughts on some of the odd beliefs I found at superstions.ca:

1. To drop your books on the way to school signifies that you will make mistakes in your lessons.
   So does leaving your books at home.
2. You must not pay the doctor entirely or there will be sickness in the family.
   Government funded medical coverage makes people sick.
3. When two persons each put one hand flat together, palm to palm, they will quarrel.
   When one person puts a fist on the cheek of another, they are already quarrelling.
4. If you bite your fingernails you will always be poor.
   The number two cause of poverty is not getting a job.
5. If you can cut a pie fair and true, you'll have a likely husband. If you make a bed handsomely, you'll have a handsome husband.

My wife cuts perfectly straight and makes a bed like no other.

6. One who habitually bites the nails is ill-natured . . .
   . . . and poor.
7. The free use of salt is a sign of having a temper . . .
   . . . and high blood pressure.
8. If you sleep with your head towards the north, it will prevent sickness.
   If you sleep with your head in a pillowcase, it will prevent breathing.
9. If the sole of either foot itches, you will walk on strange ground.
   If the sole of your foot is itching, you may already be walking on strange ground.
10. To sit on a table is a sign of coming disappointment.
    At least, it is when visiting the home of cannibals.
11. If you stub your toe going into a house, you are not wanted there.
    That's why I just let it bleed on the carpet.
12. If, in going visiting, you stub the right toe, you are welcome; if the left toe, you are unwelcome.
    That's why I only let the left one bleed.
13. Tickling a baby causes stuttering.
    What a load of crap!
    R-r-r-right, M-m-m-m-mom?
14. To twirl a chair on one leg means that you are going to fight with somebody.
    In all likelihood, it will be with the person who was sitting on the chair.

15. If two persons wash their hands at the same time, it is a sign that they will be friends forever. If two persons wipe their hands at the same time, they will be foes forever.
More relational accidents happen in the washroom than in any other room in the house.
16. Never say "goodbye" more than once.
And never *say "That dress makes you look fat"* . . . EVER!

MIDNIGHT THRILL

This morning, I got up bright and early. Okay, so it wasn't exactly bright, but it was early . . . for me.

It was 7:00 a.m.

I was thoroughly disappointed when my alarm went off, but not because it was 7:00 a.m. . . . or that it was still dark outside . . . or even that it was ice-cold in my room.

I was peeved that yet another great dream had been cut off mid-stream.I hate that! And it happens far too often. Just when things are getting good in Dreamland . . .

BEEP, BEEP, BEEP!

Actually, my alarm doesn't beep. I use my cell phone, and it plays a tune called *Memory*. It's a pleasant little ditty, but I'm thinking about replacing it with the A-Team theme song.

Anyway, just prior to being raised from the dead (of sleep), I was having one of the most incredibly awesome dreams, ever!

But sadly, and ironically, as *Memory* started to play, the memory of my dream began to fade. So, unfortunately, I can't explain all the details to you. However, I am able to recall most of it. The story seemed to revolve around free-range chickens, Abe Lincoln, and a road trip to Kamloops, BC.

Now you understand why I'm upset. I mean, seriously . . . who wouldn't want to know how that ended?

But there's no use crying about it because my alarm did go off for a reason. I had something to do. An important thing.

A thing that would make missing the end of an epic dream worthwhile.

"What thing?" you ask.

Was I going to meet Ben Stiller? Nope.

Heading off on a Caribbean cruise? Nope.

Buying new furniture from Ikea? Nope.

So then, what was this awesome reality that would, ultimately, replace my awesome dream?

It was this: I had to clean my back deck before the roofers arrived.

Yep. That's right. You heard me. No one will ever know if Abe and I arrived safely in Kamloops because I had to clean my deck!

Stupid roofers.

How frustrating.

Now, I will never know if the chickens were really secret agents, which I was beginning to suspect.

I will never know if Abe was just using me to get close to Ben Stiller, which I was also beginning to suspect.

And I will never know if the man in black, who was following us, was an assassin or just going to Kamloops as well.

This is killing me. There was so much left unsaid.

Why would Abe never take off his hat? What was he hiding?

Why was the chicken we knew as Karl carrying a passport that read "Henry"?

And where did the kilt-wearing blond girl from the McDonald's disappear to?

So many questions.

Would the eighteen-foot silver girdle turn out to be just a myth?

What does "sweet honey when the moon rises to the north" mean? And why did Abe kill the person who said it?

And how did the monkey in the Spider-Man mask crack the safe's combination so quickly?

So few answers.

Why did the raspberry smoothie taste like lemon?

How did the man in black survive the crash? I saw his car explode in flames after we ran him off the road during the long, winding chase through the mountains.

And whatever happened to the suitcase that was once handcuffed to Karl's leg?

So much mystery still to be unravelled.

Why did that small-town gas attendant slip a pack of smokes into my hand and whisper, "Three-six-nine-four"?

Would anyone ever find the all-important corner piece to that ancient map?

And for goodness sake . . . who the heck was Thomas?

What a thriller . . . but now I guess I'll never know how it ends.

Stupid roofers.

A Feverish Account

I have been sick, and I never saw it coming. Last week, I was feeling better than ever. I'm forty years old, but I didn't feel a day older than thirty-nine. I had been rising early, taking my vitamins, and faithfully doing my Wii Fit™ exercise program. In fact, I was twelve solid days into a great routine of health and fitness when . . .

WHAM!

George Michael?! What are you doing here? Let the hallucinations begin . . .

The last few days have been *very* difficult. When the strength of your youth is so suddenly stripped away, you begin to miss the little things of life — like being able to leap naked through the corn fields like a gazelle.

Oh, how I miss those days . . . although I'm not sure the old farmer with the corn field does.

Anyway, I wish I could say that I have almost been restored to full health, but that would be a lie, and I'm no liar.

A streaker, yes; a liar, no.

Although my sickly days are clearly not over — based on the constant nasal drip — I do believe I have endured the worst of it and have come through remarkably well.

Now, in my younger days, when pride ruled the heart of this awesome person called Me, I would have simply told

you that any recovery was solely due to the motivating work of my inner gladiator (he's just like me . . . only really tanned, with huge biceps and a jaw-line that would make Ryan Seacrest's face look like a circle).

However, today I acknowledge that I did not fight this fight alone. Please bear with me as I take a moment to publicly thank those who helped carry me through this dark hour, and who, I believe, also hold the keys to my ultimate victory.

Mr. Kleenex® without you I would have had to endure soggy pillows and a crusty night shirt . . . or worse. I'm no scientist, but had you not been available, Mr. Mucus may well have expanded so much that my brain exploded. I owe you my life . . . or at least the price of a new pillowcase.

Mr. Noodle, just knowing you were always only three and a half minutes away brought comfort to my soul. Your steamy broth warmed me when I was chilled, and Mr. Raw Throat was no match for your smooth noodly noodles. You were so yummy you made my tummy sing songs of joy that could be heard all the way to my colon.

Mr. Tylenol®, I needed rest and you gave me rest. With Mr. Fever attacking at a feverish rate and Mr. Headache pounding relentlessly, you surrounded me, every four hours, like a hen protecting her chick. I would not have slept so much, nor so soundly, without you. Sure, you were probably responsible for some wickedly weird dreams, but at least I slept.

Quite honestly, I wouldn't trade that one about Britney Spears fighting the giant spider for anything.

And finally, Mr. Bieber. Justin, you are my inspiration. As long as you are singing, I will . . .

Hello. Timmy's physician, Dr. Steingold, here. Timmy has just passed out from an extremely high fever.

I'm not sure Timmy was completely aware of all he just wrote; however, since it is not much different from his previous "sound mind" writings, I'll include it anyway on his behalf.

The Baby Whisperer

So, I learned something pretty cool on Friday, and it's really life-changing.

As much as I wanted to keep the information for myself, I realized how selfish that would be. So today I will reveal it to you.

Ladies and gentlemen, it is official. Babies make sounds.

Yep. They do. And from mud huts to downtown condos, this is apparently true of babies all around the world.

Now if you need to take a moment to catch your breath, do it now because that's not all. Babies make sounds that . . . wait for it . . . mean something!

Uh-huh. That's right. They talk.

It's just that, like dolphins, I have no idea what they are saying.

But Priscilla Dunstan does. Well, I'm not sure about dolphins, but she is fluent in baby talk. She's the Baby Whisperer. (That's not really her moniker. I just made it up.)

This lady traveled the globe, studying little ones and the curious utterings they produce. What she discovered was that all babies say five main words: neh, eh, eairh, heh and owh.

She has since marketed a DVD called *What 'Chu Talkin' about Willis*?

Actually, it's called *The Dunstan Baby Language*, and it trains people to hear these five baby words, thus making their parenting experience that much easier. In fact, it makes such a dramatic difference that, on the website, one lady said, "I feel like I want another child because of this."

Really? C'mon. Learning how to understand baby talk may be cool and all, but it's not like she found the secret to making them sleep through the night, walk on their own, or stop pooping themselves.

"Hey, how's parenting going?"

"Awesome! I haven't slept in three weeks, my arms and shoulders are numb, and I've got poop under my fingernails, but I know what my baby is saying. It's heaven."

So, what exactly do the babies say? Well, in no particular order, here is the translation:

"Neh" means "I'm hungry";

"Eh" means "I need to be burped";

"Eairh" means "I have gas"; and

"Owh" means "I'm tired".

Then there's "heh". I have to say that I like "heh". It means "I'm uncomfortable", which pretty much covers everything, including being hungry, having gas, and feeling tired. It's important to always have a catch-all.Whether the baby has an itch, a splinter, or a ruptured kidney, "heh" will cover it.

I don't know about you, but doesn't crying create that same sort of ambiguous reality?

This whole scenario would make a great television drama series. The following scene is from the soon-to-be-pitched-to-Fox series, *The Baby Whisperer*:

Scene:	It's early afternoon in a rustic farm house, somewhere in Middle America. A young mother is quietly washing dishes when she is startled by her three-month-old child:
Baby:	Heh.
Mom:	Lil' Billy? How'd you get here?
Baby:	Heh.
Mom:	You rode the dog? I see, but where's your brother?
Baby:	Heh.
Mom:	Timmy's in danger!?
Baby:	Heh.
Mom:	He's stuck in the well?
Baby:	Heh.
Mom:	Down at the old Jones' Farm?
Baby:	Heh.
Mom:	I'll go . . . you stay here and call 911.
Operator:	911 can I help you?
Baby:	Heh.
Operator:	Child . . . Jones's Farm . . . well . . . got it!
Baby:	Heh.
Operator:	No . . . thank YOU!

Now, don't try and tell me that wouldn't make gripping entertainment.

Well, that's all from me for now because "eiarh!"

A Moment for Eternity

Sometimes we only have a moment. Sometimes even less. What a person does with that brief window of opportunity speaks volumes about the individual . . .

. . . and makes a world of difference in the lives of others.

What would your moment say about you?

How would your moment help others?

What could you do in one minute?

Imagine if you only had one minute to share the essence of all the wisdom you've accumulated over your years?

What if you were given a mere sixty seconds to put the keys of life into the hands of someone just starting out?

What would you say?

I know what I'd say . . . now.

You see, today I asked myself those questions, and to be honest, I wasn't quite sure how I would use my moment.

So, full of curiosity, I set the timer on my phone for sixty seconds, started the countdown and, without any time to fully process my thoughts, began typing.

It was an amazing exercise.

The following is what I wrote before the beep signalled the end of my minute.

After looking it over, I'm pretty convinced my minute is packed with an eternity of wisdom:

Keep on laughin'.

Carpe diem.

In the fullness of time.

Seek first His Kingdom.

Don't wear Speedos®.

Idioms . . . with a "T"

Today, I could say I'm feeling a little under the weather, but what a stupid saying that is. "Under the weather". What does that even mean? How can someone be *under* the weather? If I were feeling healthy, I wouldn't tell you that I'm *over* the weather. That would sound silly.

"Under the weather" is what is called an idiom. And, in most cases, idiom should be spelled with a "t" instead of an "m". Here are my thoughts on some other really dumb sayings:

1. Get Your Just Desserts
   Now, if this was used in a positive sense, then it would not be on the list. However, more often than not, it is used as a threat. For example: "Hey, don't do that bad thing or you'll get your just desserts".
   There's only one person that threat would ever deter — a dead person. I mean, who doesn't love dessert?
   And if someone told me that I'm going to get *just* dessert, I'm thinking, *Sweet! Bring it on!*
   A better option might be "get your just vegetables". Then, maybe, I would think twice.
2. Say the Word
   "I'm ready to start whenever you say the word."
   What word?

What is this magical word that brings about action?

Start?

Go?

Now?

The answer is, in fact, all three . . . and a whole lot of other words.

Actually, I don't think it really matters what word is said. You could say "sheep" and probably warrant a response. In fact, I don't even think you need to *say* a word to *say the word*. I've seen a nod of the head, a finger point, and even a poorly performed Irish jig do the trick.

3. SMARTY PANTS

   Whoever came up with this idiom is a dummy-pants. It's meant to describe a person who is being a show-off and know-it-all. But connecting pants to the intellect is plain silly . . . except in the case of people who insist on wearing oversized, baggy jeans that have to be constantly pulled up. That's just not cool . . . or bright

   My son had smarty-pants once. A box of those coloured candy-coated chocolates had melted in his pocket. I quickly pointed out that chocolate mixed with heat brings about a melting effect. Mr. Smarty-Pants, I am.

4. COST AN ARM AND A LEG

   How expensive is an arm and a leg? Well, recently someone told me they were looking to buy a large screen TV which was going to cost exactly that. So, apparently, the going rate for an arm and a leg is about $2,496 plus tax. The obvious flaw in this idiom is that we have no way of knowing how much an individual arm or leg would cost, which renders comparison shopping almost impossible. However, after doing some research, here's what I do know. At Wal-Mart, one arm and one leg can buy you a 52 inch LCD HDTV. If you chose, instead, to purchase two electric scooters, with helmets, you'd probably get a knee back in change.

And if you really wanted to go big, you could enjoy a 1999 Beetle hatchback with 141,000 km on the clock. Of course, to make that deal, you'd have to render yourself completely limbless . . . so it may not be the best trade-off

5. HOT POTATO

Everyone wants to avoid a hot potato because it is one of many dangerous topics which will, inevitably, cause families, communities and nations to crumble.

Now, I have actually touched a hot potato before. It was fresh from the oven, with the foil still wrapped around it. I will not lie . . . it was definitely hot. But it certainly wasn't hot enough to send me into the fetal position every time I saw a potato after that.

Surely, to describe such sensitive issues, someone could have come up with a more feared item than the potato — hot or not. Try "mother-in-law".

6. RIDE THE GRAVY TRAIN

Ewww! I've heard someone say, "If only I were rich, then I'd be riding the gravy train." Well, if I was rich, I wouldn't. That's gross.

How in the world did riding a train of gravy become a symbol of luxury? Let the poor slop around in it instead. I understand the importance of making achievable goals,

but gravy being the ultimate success story? You might as well call it the plum sauce train. A nice extra, but not where I hope to settle.
Of course, it could be that the phrase is just trying to compare the smooth flow of gravy with the ease of living. If so, the person who coined this idiom has obviously never experienced the lumpy gravy that has marked many a meal in my lifetime.

Well, there you have it. Some idioms with a "t". I have to admit, when I first started writing this article I was banging my head against a brick wall. But then the words just flowed like a river, and everything has come up roses. As a result, I've turned 180 degrees and feel like a million dollars.

Inside the Writer's Mind

Writing is thirty percent grammar, thirty percent spelling, eighty percent good idea . . . and zero percent math.

As a writer, the number one question I am asked is: "What do you think about when you're writing such deep inspirational material?"

Actually, that may be the *best* question asked, but the most popular question is: "What makes *you* think you're a writer?" But it doesn't really matter. The point is, when it comes to writing, the reader always sees the finished product. They very rarely get a glimpse of the process behind the product. Even when they do get the opportunity to watch a writer work at their craft, the reader still doesn't see what's going on in the writer's mind.

So, what do I think while I write?

Well, I am about to become the Penn & Teller of writers, as I lift the veil to reveal the inner workings of my mind whilst in the performance of literary magic.

ENTER MY THINK TANK.

What to write.

What to write.

Hmm.... How about the faked moon landing? Yeah, that's good. Conspiracy theories are in. So . . .

I believe the moon landing was faked.

Really? That's how you're going to start? I believe the moon landing was faked? C'mon man! You need something to really grab the reader's attention. Something to draw them in. It needs to make your belief known, but be written cryptically. Obvious, but coy. Think moon landing. Think pop culture . . . I got it! How about:

One small step for man; one giant leap for mankind. What a load of—

Hold on! Watch your words there. It has to be something strong enough to drive your point home, but without crossing a line and driving readers away. Hmm . . . What a load of baloney? Hooey? Cheese?

What? Cheese? Seriously, what kind of message does "what a load of cheese" send?

If you're going to take on such a polarizing subject you may as well just go for it. Let it all hang out. Take the bull by the horns and shake things up. Like:

What a load of poo-poo!

Yes! That's it. Now we're onto something. Oh wait, I've got a better one.

One small step for man; one giant leap for mankind. Right into a pile of poo-poo!

Funny, but scandalous. It's brilliant, but maybe there should be a twist at the beginning . . .

Did I change the kitty litter? I can't remember. Oh well, I can't check now. I'm on a roll. In the zone.

Focus, man. Focus!

Where was I?

Step. Leap. Poo. Twist.

Right . . . the twist. It needs a little something to completely throw readers off, and then . . . BOOM!

Drop the faked moon landing right in their lap! Yeah, that's sweet. Let's start like:

We live in a world that has no boundaries . . .

Now that's deep stuff. Pulitzer Prize stuff. Then I'll add:

Or so they say.

Wow, I just got chills. Or . . . so . . . they . . . say. Oh yeah. It turns from optimistic to ominous in a split second.

Okay, with the reader in a daze from that spectacular literary uppercut, it's time to drop the bomb.

Awesome.

Well, that's it. It doesn't matter what I write from this point. The reader is there for the long haul.

EXIT MY THINK TANK.

There you have it folks. It may be just two lines, but now you've seen the thought process behind the written words I'm sure you'll really appreciate the magic that appears before you.

We live in a world that has no boundaries. Or so they say. One small step for man; one giant leap for mankind. Right into a pile of poo-poo!

Oh, baby. The world may never truly be ready to handle what flows from this mind.

And to think my mom wanted me to go into mathematics.

JURY DUTY . . . OR NOT

Today I went to court. I was in the final grouping of potential jurors for what has the makings of being a long trial. So I rose early this morning, kissed my wife goodbye (long and passionate . . . as usual), finished filling out my juror questionnaire (with the whole truth and nothing but the truth), and headed off to the courthouse.

Upon arrival—after going through metal detectors, riding four escalators, and visiting the bathroom—I was greeted with the following words: "Good news! The jury was selected yesterday. You can go home."

I handed in my papers and left.

A quick calculation of lost time and expenses incurred for the day revealed:

* Travel time:	1 hour 45 minutes
* Sleep deprivation:	2 hours
* Transit fares:	$6.00
* Banana bread(*to get change for transit on the way there*):	$2.00
* Hot chocolate (*to get change for transit on the way back*):	$3.26
* Stress of coping with possibility of being selected:	Immeasurable

* Total lawsuit currently pending against the Toronto court system for accumulated losses and emotional strain: $6, 000,011.26

It would have been cheaper for them to call my house.

FOH-NIKS SUX

I homeschool my children, and a few years back I spent many hours drilling the sounds, special sounds and rules of phonics into my daughter's brain.

Sometimes, when tears of frustration were in her eyes, I would say, "Sweetie, if you can just memorize these rules, you'll be able to read *anything*."

Now, phonics is a phenomenal learning tool, but it would be even more phenomenal if the rules actually applied to more than one percent of our words. Many a conversation went something like this:

ME:	When there are two vowels in a word, the second one is silent and the first one is long. Spell "made".
DAUGHTER:	M-A-D-E.
ME:	Yes! What does this spell? H-O-U-N-D?
DAUGHTER:	Honed.
ME:	No.
DAUGHTER:	But the first vowel is —
ME:	The rule doesn't apply here. It is the word "hound". O-U makes an OW sound. What does this spell? T-O-U-R.
DAUGHTER:	Tower.

Me:	No. It is the word "tour". Sometimes the sound OO is spelled O-U. Let's try another one. What does this spell? T-O-O-T-H.
Daughter:	Towth.
Me:	No. O-O is pronounced OO, as well. What does this spell? L-O-O-K.
Daughter:	Luke.
Me:	No. Sometimes O-O makes a different sound. Do you think you have it?
Daughter:	Yep.
Me:	Spell "cow".
Daughter:	C-O-U.
Me:	No. The OW sound is spelled O-W.
Daughter:	I thought it was spelled O-U?
Me:	Only sometimes.
Daughter:	When?
Me:	I'm not sure. Let's move on. Spell "bowl".
Daughter:	B-O-L-E.
Me:	No. In that word, even though there is no second vowel, the O is long and the W is silent. Spell "toll".
Daughter:	T-O-W-L.
Me:	No. That would be towel.
Daughter:	So, towel is spelled T-O-W-L?
Me:	Well, no. Towel is actually spelled T-O-W-E-L. Sometimes an E-L makes an L sound at the end of a word. Spell "bottle".
Daughter:	B-A-W-T-E-L.

ME:	No. It's L then E. and the AW sound is actually just the letter O.
DAUGHTER:	But there are two vowels.
ME:	Correct, but only one for each syllable. Let's try again. Spell "bottle".
DAUGHTER:	B-O-T-L-E.
ME:	No. There are two Ts. Spell "tinted".
DAUGHTER:	T-I-N-T-T-E-D.
ME:	No.
DAUGHTER:	But I did the short i.
ME:	Yes, but you only need one T. Okay . . . let's go in a different direction. What does this spell? N-U-R-S-E.
DAUGHTER:	Nurse.
ME:	Yes! Spell "bird".
DAUGHTER:	B-U-R-D.
ME:	No. some words use I-R and others use U-R.
DAUGHTER:	Which one does fern use?
ME:	Neither. You know what, let's go back to basics. Spell "boy".
DAUGHTER:	B-O-Y.
ME:	Spell "toy".
DAUGHTER:	T-O-Y.
ME:	No.
DAUGHTER:	It's wrong?
ME:	No. I just don't think you should spell "boy toy". Moving on. Spell "oil".
DAUGHTER:	O-Y-L.
ME:	No.

DAUGHTER: What's wrong with spelling "oil"?
ME: Nothing, but it is spelled O-I, not O-Y. Spell "knot" (the type you tie).
DAUGHTER: N-O-T.
ME: No. The K is silent, like in knight.
DAUGHTER: Night is spelled with a K?
ME: Yep . . . unless you're talking about the other night.
DAUGHTER: Like, "day and night" night?
ME: There's no K in that one. It's in words like knife, kneel, knit—
DAUGHTER: And noodle!
ME: No. Spell "keep".
DAUGHTER: K-E-P-E.
ME: No. This word has the second vowel side by side with the first, instead of at the end.
Spell "seep".
DAUGHTER: S-E-E-P.
ME: Yes! Spell "city".
DAUGHTER: S-I—
ME: No. It starts with a C.
DAUGHTER: Okay then, C-I-T . . .
ME: Yes . . . ?
DAUGHTER: Hmm. Well, if I put an E on the end, then the I becomes short.
ME: Yes . . . ?
DAUGHTER: Wouldn't that make it site?
ME: No. Site starts with an S. The end of city is actually a Y.

DAUGHTER:	So Y makes an EE sound?
ME:	Yep, that's right. So does E-E, E-A, I-E and E-Y. For example, E-A-R spells ear. So, what does this spell? B-E-A-R.
DAUGHTER:	Beer.
ME:	No. In this case, E-A-R makes an AIR sound. What does this spell? E-A-R-T-H.
DAUGHTER:	Airth?
ME:	No. Sometimes E-A-R makes an UR sound.
DAUGHTER:	Like I-R . . . and U-R?
ME:	And E-R, yes. Want to move on to suffixes?
DAUGHTER:	No.
ME:	Spell "whale".
DAUGHTER:	W-A-L-E.
ME:	No. There's an H. Spell "who".
DAUGHTER:	H-O-O.
ME:	No. There's a W. Both words start with W-H, but they make different sounds.
DAUGHTER:	Can I go to bed now?
ME:	Sure you can. Just one more. Spell "giant".
DAUGHTER:	J-I-A-N-T.
ME:	No. Good night.

It really is amazing any of us ever learned to read! Thu Ing-lish lang-gwij sux!

"T" is for Tim Hortons

Well, here I am spending another evening in Tim Hortons — Canada's favourite coffee stop. Now that the summer is over, this will be a weekly experience. So, I've decided to dedicate some writing time to my home away from home.

Using the letters in its name, here are the words that come to mind when I think of Tim Hortons:

Timbits®

What an awesome invention. It's the ultimate example of recycling. Doughnut holes becoming their own little treat. But they are also incredibly dangerous.

You see, when visiting a Tim's, most people I know would never order two doughnuts for themselves . . . because that seems a little over the top. But almost every one of those same people (including me) wouldn't think twice about finishing off a box of Timbits®. Now, I don't know for sure, but I'd bet ten Timbits® is pretty close to two doughnuts, if not more.

A deceptive little treat, but oh so good!

Institution

By "institution", I don't mean a respected place of learning or commerce, but rather the kind made to house the "crazies"!

If you've spent any time hanging out in a coffee shop — any coffee shop — you'll know what I mean. In fact, I have a prime example sitting next to me right now. The guy is muttering something about meeting somebody here, and he is a little concerned that his buddy won't find any place to park. Apparently, his friend's flying saucer is quite large.

Maple leafs

Contrary to popular belief, Tim Hortons is not some fancy name for doughnut. The franchise was founded by a real man named Tim Horton.

Seriously . . . I wouldn't make this up.

The connection with the Toronto Maple Leafs starts with the fact that Tim played part of his Hall of Fame ice hockey career with that organization — but it doesn't end there.

You see, Tim Hortons and the Maple Leafs each have a widely recognized brand, have a rabid fan base, and are moneymaking machines. However, there is one area that Tim Hortons has the edge. Both fan bases desperately want to win something big, but the coffee shop's giveaway initiative, Rrroll Up The Rim, clearly has the best odds.

Heidi

Tim Hortons is synonymous with coffee . . . and so is my wife. She loves her coffee. In fact, Heidi openly admits that it is a need, and Tim Hortons is like her dealer.

Those refillable travel mugs are a great idea and all, but if they ever come out with the Tim Hortons Intravenous Drip — cha-ching! Those would be harder to find than a Cabbage Patch Kid® in the '80s.

Open

Does this place ever close? Nope. Tim Hortons is actually open 25-7. I don't know how they do it.

But the word "open" isn't solely limited to its hours of operation. It also refers to some of the people who have sat beside me while I was hanging out there. These people are *way* too open for my liking.

Seriously, it is really hard to enjoy your doughnut when there's an older gentleman telling you about the rash he's developing on his thigh.

Rrroll Up The Rim to Win®

I hate those commercials that imply being able to properly say "rrroll up the rim" is evidence of your Canadian heritage. I find it very difficult to roll up the actual rim on my cup, let alone roll that "r" when I speak.

Rolling the rim at Tim Hortons is a Canadian tradition, along the same lines as receiving a fortune cookie at the end of a meal in a Chinese restaurant. Except, instead of reading: "You are about to meet a horrible fate", the Timmy's customer gets: "Try Again".

Equally bad news to each recipient.

Third World

For the cost of a small Tim Hortons coffee a day, a family in a developing country could have access to food, water, education, medical supplies, and small business training.

If all the regular customers gave up just one visit a day and used the money to sponsor a child, just imagine the number of lives that would change!

Opium

Poppies are, apparently, the source of opium. They are also the source of poppy seeds. I wonder how many poppy seed bagels one would need to eat in order to get high? I know it's more than six because I'm presently starting my seventh and there isn't the slightest buzz.

NET GAIN

Is there any greater racket, in the known universe, than selling a coffee and donut combo for more than two dollars? That profit margin is ridiculous!

The only thing comparable is my son selling lemonade on the street for fifty cents a glass. That kid has some deep pockets, especially since I taught him how to use his cuteness — those bright eyes and big smile — to draw in the women. He's such a little charmer . . . and budding entrepreneur.

SACRED COW

Tim Hortons is a treasured piece of Canadiana. It ranks anywhere from first to fourth on the "What is Canadian" list, depending on where you place Anne Murray, Molson Canadian®, and the beaver.

As a national icon, Timmy's is above reproach. To speak against it would be something akin to raining fire and brimstone down upon yourself. Of course, Canadians, being Canadian, would probably just give you a stern look of disgust . . . but like a *really, really* stern look.

Well, there you have it. Timmy Hortons through the eyes of Timmy Boyle.

Wisdom from a New Forty-Year-Old

Yes, I have recently turned forty . . . and proud of it. There was a time, during the peak of my youth, when I would look upon a forty-year-old individual and marvel.

"How are they still alive!?"

Well, I have entered my fifth decade, alive and well.

Although my hair has thinned, receded ever so slightly, and now sports a touch of grey, I am still more than capable, if I so choose, of growing a very big '80s mullet.

Take that, young me!

Now, for those who don't feel the status of one's hair is the ultimate assessment of graceful ageing, I present the following argument:

You don't know squat!

Not only am I very proud of turning forty, I am eagerly anticipating the next decade and all it has to offer. That being physical and mental wellness wrapped neatly in four decades of acquired wisdom.

At ten years old, I thought I had figured it all out . . .

. . . but I was wrong.

At twenty years old, I thought I had figured it all out . . .

. . . but I was wrong.

At thirty years old, I thought I had figured it all out . . .

. . . but I was wrong.

At forty years old, *I know* I've figured it all out.

I've heard the Negative Nancys say things like:

"It's all down hill from here."

"Forty is the new sixty."

"Your hair has receded more than 'slightly', you know."

But I refuse to listen. You see, Negative Nancys who sit on the younger side of thirty are perceptionally challenged, while those on the "mature" side fall into various levels of what most experts (mainly me) refer to as "bitterness".

The thirty-year-old Negative Nancy is nervously bitter about eventually turning forty.

The forty-year-old Negative Nancy is angrily bitter about having turned forty.

The fifty-year-old Negative Nancy is sarcastically bitter about passing forty.

The over sixty-year-old Negative Nancy is still bitter . . . but no longer remembers why.

I have no time to listen to bitter souls. I'm convinced life begins at forty. Therefore, by using all of the lessons I have learned, I plan on maximizing every moment of the one hundred and thirty years I have left on this planet.

Kids (which is anyone under forty), come gather round. After compiling four hundred and eighty months of life experience, here are Timmy's Top Fifty Life Truths:

1. Life is great! Bumps.Yep. Valleys.Yep. Curves. Yep. Still great.
2. Treat everyone with respect. They may be your future boss . . . or spouse . . . or science fair partner.

3. Never waste too much time doing something you hate. So, if you don't like reading this list, get out now!
4. Political correctness sucks. (Can I say that?)
5. If you've never failed . . . you've failed. Which, ironically, would make you a success.
6. Kiss Negative Nancys goodbye . . . and don't let the door hit them on the way out.
7. Always carry pen and paper . . . because technology, at times, sucks more than political correctness.
8. Carpe diem!
9. Learn Latin if you don't know what carpe diem means.
10. Speedos® are never the right answer. *Never.*
11. Laughter is an amazing gift. Don't let it gather dust.
12. Parenting is way easier than we make it out to be.
    Rule #1: Love your kid.
    Rule #2: See Rule #1.
13. Embrace silence. It's amazing what you hear when there is no sound.
14. Desire authenticity, but understand everybody needs to wear a mask occasionally . . . even if it is just for Comic Con.
15. Trustworthiness and teachability will always break the tie in academic equality.
16. True freedom is found within reasonable restrictions.
17. Respect your elders . . . especially those who just turned forty.
18. Learn from the past . . . or your future won't look any better than your present.
19. The customer is always valued . . . but not always right.

20. It never hurts to ask, unless you ask to get hit.
21. Don't hide the knife; Teach how to use the knife responsibly.
22. Life doesn't move quickly. You do. Slow down.
23. Remember: When you pray for rain, someone else might be praying for sunshine.
24. Celebrities pick their nose hairs one at a time, just like you and me.
25. Sometimes it looks better on paper . . . especially graph paper.
26. You need way less than you think you need, unless you think you only need marshmallows.
27. Have a plan, but don't forget to plan for your plan to change unplanned.
28. Nothing happens overnight . . . except dew.
29. Don't have regrets; have life lessons.
30. Eat when you're hungry. Drink when you're thirsty. Minimize the sugar.
31. Don't take medication for problems that a change in lifestyle can fix.
32. Dance like no one is watching. Better yet, take time to dance when no one is watching.
33. Wear sunscreen.
34. Don't blame God (or life) for things you have brought on yourself.
35. Boxer shorts cover more skin than swim suits. Take your morning walks proudly.
36. Be a generous tipper.
37. Dare 2 Dream!
38. Relationships over anything else. All the time.

39. Change what you can; accept what you can't. (P.S. you can't change your spouse.)
40. These three remain: faith, hope and love. None of them have failed me yet.
41. The best drivers assume the other drivers around them are idiots . . . and could change lanes at any minute.
42. The #1 waste of time is not television or Facebook. It's worry! So . . . don't . . . worry. Watch *The A-Team*.
43. Money is not evil. However, those new Canadian plastic bills are pure sin.
44. Be proactive . . . or at least react by being proactive.
45. The '80s rocked. Long live neon.
46. There is someone for everyone. Think of anyone. Yes, even them. Weird but true.
47. You have to know when to hold, fold, walk, and run. Ask Kenny. He'll confirm it.
48. Speaking of Kenny, it is possible to get too much "work" done.
49. No matter how old you get, fart jokes and "bleeping" will always make you laugh.
50. To "assume" doesn't make a "bleep" out of you and me. It puts the "bleep" in front of you and me.

And remember, I'm *not* old. I'm only forty . . . not fifty.

The Oscar Goes to . . . Flannelgraph Clooney

On Sunday, the red carpet was rolled out and the Hollywood stars gathered together. It was such an awesome moment. There wasn't a dry glass in the house.

Well, my good friend Diane wrote a great post on the unnecessary extravagance that is the *Academy Awards*. All that pomp and pageantry seems a bit much in light of all the needs around the world . . . and the many celebrity-philanthropists who attend these festivities.

Now, I'm all for throwing a great party, making great money, and honouring great performances, but I also understand the need for balance and perspective in the process. So, after reading Diane's thoughts and statistical breakdown of Oscar's expenses, I began thinking about ways to make this Hollywood gala more financially and socially responsible.

Here's the plan for next year: The organizers and invitees set their budgets, as they would under normal circumstances, and then save as much money as possible. Any unspent budget money is donated to a deserving charity. So, here are five ways to save money on next year's Oscars:

1. Car Pool

   Forget the individual limos. Everybody meet at Ben Stiller's palatial estate, say around 4:00 p.m., and hop on the Oscar Bus. Once the last celebrity is aboard, Ty Pennington will yell "Move that bus!" and they'll be red carpet bound.

Some might say, "How are you going to get all those celebs on one bus?"

Have you seen some of those actresses? They'll fit.

2. Surprise Bags

Everyone will still get a gift bag. Except now, instead of Cadillac rides, boxing training sessions, and BlackBerries, it will be filled with stuff they'll actually use, like gum, squirt guns, and marbles.

"And the winner is..." won't be nearly as exciting as hearing, "What did you get?"

3. Flannelgraph

Sure, the flash and dazzle of an intricate light show, woven seamlessly into an elaborate song and dance number, perfectly choreographed to accompanying videos, is highly entertaining, but seriously . . . you telling me a well-planned Flannelgraph display can't accomplish the same thing? My Sunday School teacher would beg to differ.

Who needs 3-D when you can walk through the history of cinema on an easel? And wouldn't a young Liz Taylor look hot in felt.

4. Go Nude

Why do people wear such extravagant outfits when Oscar's statue is standing, for obvious reasons, behind a strategically placed sword?

If you replace "Best & Worst Dressed" with "Best & Worst Undressed", you'll not only save a ton of money, but send already high television ratings through the roof . . . and the roof above that. I haven't watched the Oscars in years, but count me in on this one.

"I only watch the Oscars for the speeches."

4. HIRE ME TO HOST

   I don't know what fee or perks an Oscar Host gets, but I'd do it for FREE, and I certainly won't do any worse than some of the lame ducks they've put on that stage over the last few years.

So there we have it—a no-frills evening. Money saved. People helped. Chocolate statues enjoyed by all.

Why Are You Here?

If you arc reading these final words, one of the following has occurred:

1. You have opened the book backwards . . . and possibly upside down.
   Turn it over and start at the real beginning.
2. You have turned to the last page just to see who the murderer is.
   (It was the butler's butler.)
3. You have skimmed the book hoping it gets better.
   Now that you've found out it does, go back and soak it all in, properly.
4. You have successfully navigated and enjoyed the craziness *Inside Timmy's Mind*.
   Go tell the world, but remember, although I mentioned at the beginning that you can't catch insanity . . . I'm no doctor.
   Good luck.

Want More? See Timmy in 3-D

I hope you have enjoyed this book as much as I enjoyed writing the stories it contains. There are very few things in life which bring me more joy than giving people the gift of laughter.

In 2009, I launched *Up Standing Comedy* with the desire to provide an "upstanding" comedy experience—through video, writing and live performance—that is high in quality, clean in content, and genuinely me.

If you have been entertained by my unique perspective as presented on the preceding pages, then experience Timmy in 3-D by bringing me to your stage.

> "Classic stand-up comedy, without the rude and crude, enables everyone the opportunity to share, together, in the gift that is . . . laughter!"
>
> — Timmy

For more information about how you can provide the gift of laughter to your community, church, campus, or corporate gathering, visit me at upstandingcomedy.ca or email me at timmyboyle@upstandingcomedy.ca

Printed in the USA
CPSIA information can be obtained
at www.ICGtesting.com
JSHW021537251024
72385JS00001B/2

9 781922 135025